ACPL ITEM
DISCARDED

11-30-61
2-20-62

MID-CENTURY ARCHITECTURE IN AMERICA

MID-CENTURY ARCHITECTURE IN AMERICA

Honor Awards of the American Institute of Architects, 1949-1961

Foreword by PHILIP WILL, Jr., FAIA

Edited and with an Introduction by WOLF VON ECKARDT

THE JOHNS HOPKINS PRESS, BALTIMORE

© 1961, The American Institute of Architects, Washington, D. C.
Distributed in Great Britain by Oxford University Press, London

Design and layout by Edward D. King
Typography by Monotype Composition Company
Printed in the United States of America by Universal Lithographers, Inc.
Binding by Moore and Company

Library of Congress Card Catalog Number 61-17081

FOREWORD

Philip Will, Jr., President of the AIA

1166609

IN THESE PAGES, the reader is invited to examine the buildings which architects have judged to be among the best American architecture created during the past twelve years. The Honor Awards program of The American Institute of Architects is dedicated to the encouragement of distinguished design. It also serves each year to give recognition to that work.

Yet this is only part of the meaning of the AIA Honor Awards, as a study of the winning designs from 1949 through 1961 will reveal. It is a striking representation of where architecture stands today as a full-blown American art and where it promises to lead.

The importance of this exposition is not limited to the architect, whose natural preoccupation is design; to the fellow artist in allied fields; or to the critic or dilettante. Architecture is more than an art, though it is regarded as the mother of the family of fine arts, without which life would have little joy or meaning. It is more than engineering, which supports our structures, spans our waterways, and promises to carry man to the moon. It is far more than construction, which assembles materials for shelter.

It is the making and re-making of the physical environment in which we live, work, play, study, worship, and love. It is the design of a single room and the re-shaping of a huge city. It gives comfort and pleasure to a child and vitality and beauty to a nation.

These are reasons why architecture is important to every American. Yet there is one more, and it is the reason why this book has been produced. It is the new role of the ordinary citizen in our new age of architecture.

We face the biggest building boom in any nation's history. The forces behind it—the rapid expansion of our population and the growing obsolescence of our cities—are irresistible. The question is not whether we will build on an unprecedented scale but how well we will do it. We can either create a new nation of social purpose, riches, and beauty to outshine the glories of Greece and Rome, or we can erect the most chaotic and wasteful urban civilization which man's innate capacity for folly can devise.

The power to do either lies, only in small part, with the architect. Although, as designer and co-ordinator of professions and trades, he decides *how* and sometimes *where* to build, he seldom decides *what* and *when*. These decisions are made by the client. In past ages, the clients of architecture were government and the church. The temple, the tomb, the palace, the castle, and the cathedral were architectural expressions of other eras and the focal points of their communities. These expressions were ordered by a few and fixed in the accepted design principles and technology of the times. Even in nineteenth-century America, the man of wealth served as the principal client of architecture in commissioning our early office buildings, industrial plants, mansions, and country estates.

Today, the monarchs and fixed orders are gone and our technology is limitless. Our new architecture is an architecture of democracy, in which every building has a contribution to make to its owner and the community in the complex urban design of the twentieth-century life.

The new client of this new architecture is the ordinary citizen. As owner, he is responsible for his house; as parent and taxpayer, for his school; as parishioner, for his church; as trustee, investor, and committeeman, for bank, factory, and office building—and, as voter and constituent, for the massive urban design and re-design of our cities and towns. Within 40 years, we will have to duplicate every single structure in the nation—in effect, build a second United States—to accommodate a population which will nearly double in that time.

As architects, we have been through major design revolutions which have given us the capacity to enrich human life as never before. Though as individuals we treat our design problems differently, our profession today has a common aim. We see our new architecture as an art aimed at satisfying social needs. We define function not in terms of visual effect but as the arrangement and enclosure of spaces to make human activities more productive and enjoyable. We consider materials as tools for enclosure, not as symbolic labels for fixed styles. Engineering we use as a means to appropriate structure, not for structural exhibitionism. And in our new architecture, conceived on whatever scale, we are conscious of the need to relate our buildings to the size and perspective of people, with renewed attention to man's natural love for that warmth, texture, and decoration which he associates with beauty.

How this force for great accomplishment will be utilized in the immediate years ahead depends on the level of understanding of the citizen of today. This book shows examples of what the architectural profession is capable of offering. We do not expect it to revolutionize taste or provoke public acclaim. If it will make one small step toward better understanding we will be satisfied.

CONTENTS

INTRODUCTION

by Wolf Von Eckardt

THE TWENTIETH-CENTURY REVOLUTION IN ARCHITECTURE has been accomplished," Henry R. Luce told the centennial convention of The American Institute of Architects in 1957. "And it has been accomplished mainly in America—no matter how great our debt to European genius."

This accomplishment comes at a providential time, the Editor-in-Chief of *Time* added, "precisely at the moment when there is taking place, and is about to take place, the most staggering mass of building ever done on this planet."

To accommodate our exploding population and to arrest the decay of our cities, we in this country will build as much again by the end of the century as we have built in our entire history as a nation. The shape of these second United States is largely foreshadowed by the buildings shown in this book—a comprehensive survey of America's new architecture.

The battle for this architecture which, for lack of a better word, we generally call "modern," was largely won by the time the AIA honor award program got under way in 1949. But the honored buildings in this book are neither avant-garde nor merely typical. The twelve juries of outstanding architects, who selected them over as many years from among several thousand entries, did not intend to prove the virtue of any "style."

Neither do AIA juries favor one particular method of construction or school of design. They seek to honor only what they, as architects and critics, consider architectural distinction. They look for excellence and for "well building," as the English writer and diplomat Sir Henry Wotton put it in 1624, which, he said, "hath three conditions: commodity, firmness and delight."

Sir Henry harbored no doubts how, in his time and place, "well building" was to be properly expressed. Inigo Jones had just accomplished *his* architectural revolution in England upon discovering what the great Andrea Palladio had, half a century earlier, discovered about the architecture of antiquity. Three hundred years later, sundry versions of Palladian palaces, along with Roman baths, Gothic cathedrals, and colonial mansions, were still rising—quite firmly, to be sure, more rarely delightful, and hardly ever commodiously—to house industrialists, railroad stations, skyscrapers, and even factories. They rose all over the Western world from Aachen to Atlanta, in self-righteous disregard of indigenous culture, natural terrain, native materials, technological advance, and local climate.

The search for a new architecture started mostly in protest against the absurd anachronism of these archeological exercises. It began, as the art historian S. Giedion points out, in opposition to "an infected atmosphere and as a moral revolt against the falsification of forms" in the Victorian era.

At first it seemed as though the only alternative to masquerading buildings in historic costumes was to present them in a state of pristine nudity. But that was by no means all there was to it. For architecture moves forward only when new demands on "commodity" are met by new ways of providing "firmness," and both combine to answer new concepts of "delight." A new architecture combines new usefulness with new construction methods in the creation of new forms.

The pioneers of the new architecture have often quoted a remark by Eugène Viollet-le-Duc, the French architect and restorer of Notre Dame in Paris and other cathedrals: Gothic, he said a hundred years or so ago, "is not the result of a caprice any more than it is only a decorative expression. It is, if you wish, a necessity of the structure." It is that, to be sure. But Gothic painting and sculpture are imbued with the same spirit and spirituality as the cathedrals. This the early modernists overlooked when they cited Viollet-le-Duc to support their contention that the appearance of their buildings was determined by structural necessity alone. There are no steel girders in Piet Mondrian's paintings, which had such a decisive influence on early modern architecture, particularly that of de Stijl group. Nor did the form of early modern buildings, or any buildings for that matter, follow function alone, no matter how often Louis Sullivan's phrase is quoted. Good form does follow function *and* structural necessity *and* artistic caprice, if you wish to call it that. All three combine in an expression of civilization at one moment in history. "It is not the whim or desire of the architect," says art historian R. Furneaux Jordan, "that brings about the cathedral, but organized Christendom and the craft-guilds, the monastic and feudal systems." It has been thus for three-thousand years of Western architecture.

The architects of ancient Egypt protected their royal tombs against pilferage, time, and the desert with the simplest possible post and lintel construction and the intent to create a deliberately awesome monument. Their monuments were monuments and have lasted these three-thousand years because of that. It would seem doubtful that we, today, would care much about the great Ramses II or his period, had his admirers honored him with a children's hospital or a school for foreign service officers.

The Greeks built temple-shrines for their holy statues by placing pitched roofs of wood framing over columns. As in their sculpture, they achieved an unsurpassed refinement of balance and proportion—an inimitable beauty we shall never cease to admire. The Romans needed larger interior spaces. They achieved it with the arch and with their invention of the concrete vault. Their architecture was meant to, and did, impress their entire world with imperial dignity and splendor.

A circular arrangement of arches resulted in the dome and the inspired and inspiring feat of engineering and beauty of such early medieval structures as Hagia Sophia at Istanbul. And as the arch became pointed—an ingenious accomplishment of stone engineering—it was used together with the new invention of stained glass in an intricate skeleton frame which made the Gothic cathedrals possible. The Renaissance, some two-hundred years later, combined and perfected all these structural systems and architectural forms and subordinated them to its revolution in thought, its new learning, and its veneration of man and his genius.

The machine age suddenly brought not only new needs for housing industry and mechanized transportation, but also new building materials—iron, steel, and reinforced concrete—and hence new construction methods. Nineteenth-century architects used both but bashfully hid them within structures which only pretended to the style of earlier ways of building. For the concept of "delight" changed more slowly. It was not until there emerged the artistic intent to create an architecture appropriate to the new needs and uses and to a new way of life and thought that architects noticed what the engineers had already accomplished. Joseph Paxton's Crystal Palace in London of 1851, Gustave Eiffel's famous tower in Paris in 1889, and Robert Maillart's graceful and daring reinforced concrete bridges in Switzerland are but the most outstanding of these pioneering accomplishments.

The new structures did away with the old stone and brick architecture which, in unending variety, piled horizontal upon vertical elements so that they best supported each other. Steel and reinforced concrete made a radically new development possible, first accomplished in Chicago in 1885. There, William Le Baron Jenny, instead of letting the walls carry themselves and the weight of all the floors for the full height of his Home Insurance Building, let a steel frame do the job. The walls of the steel "cage" now became mere "curtains" to keep out rain, wind, and noise. Such "curtain walls" are still undergoing a flurry of new developments in steel, aluminum, porcelain enamel, glass, and other materials in all manner of color and design.

At first, honest and overt expression of this new building technique was almost exclusively confined to industrial buildings. Factories and warehouses cried out for new forms and, tucked away in industrial districts and suburbs, these new forms were least apt to outrage a citizenry still happy with the old pseudo-cathedrals and fake Palladian mansions.

Not so the avant-garde of the new art and architecture. Art Nouveau was a brief and often creative period of transition. But its "flowing and sinuous yet oddly limp" decorations (art critic John Canaday's phrase) lost all meaning in the Armageddon of World War I and the cultural and social upheaval it pointed up. The German historian Egon Friedell saw the cause of this upheaval in "the collapse of reality." Whether artists studied Einstein or not, they sensed with the intuitive perception of their calling that the sky above was no longer a shelter but infinite and that all is relative. Whether artists read Freud or even heard of him, they knew that man's behavior was no longer determined by reason alone but by the depth of the subconscious as well, by the stuff that dreams are made of.

Artists felt they could no longer render the meaning of this new world in representational terms as through the lens of a camera. Human aspirations and anxieties, as their art revealed them, could no longer be expressed by unclad maidens basking in the light. Some, like Paul Klee with his whimsical paintings, took flight into non-objective fancy. Others, like Picasso in his "Guernica," depicted the state of man in tortured outcries. Still others, like Mondrian with his geometric compositions, engaged in a desperate search for the essence of harmony and order. Art tried to capture motion, as did Duchamp in "Nude Descending a Staircase"; or the simultaneousness of things, as did Gropius when, in his Fagus factory, he showed the interior and exterior at the same time through a glass wall; or the mechanical precision of a machine part, as did Brancusi with his sculpture "Bird in Space." Artists constructed and abstracted and—for a fleeting moment—became obsessed with the fancied virtue of the machine. For the machine promised them not only abundant production and thus social justice but also a new aesthetic. It seemed to make everything possible except the continuance of a tradition which now seemed not only meaningless but decadent.

Thus the German architect Hans Poelzig sketched his visions of re-shaping the Alps. "Man multiplied by the motor, alone with the stokers who sweat before the satanic furnaces of great ships, alone with the black phantoms who ferret in red-hot bellies of locomotives as they hurtle forward at insensate speeds," said the Italian poet of "Futurism," Filippo Tommaso Marinetti, could no longer live, let alone be depicted in classic repose. The machine, said the Dutch painter-architect, Theo van Doesburg, "stands in the forefront of our cultural will to create a style." And the painter-sculptor-poet-architect-planner Le Corbusier, who thirty years later was to create such emotional architecture, proclaimed at the time that a house should be a machine á habiter.

Architect Peter Blake holds that what "Corbu" really meant was "a house should be as beautiful as a machine," and not necessarily as coldly efficient. But isn't that what the others meant, too, when for that brief spell the modern movement was infatuated by "machine art"? At any rate, architects soon recognized what is still the central problem of architecture today: whether man or machine is to be the master.

For the machine only reproduces what man creates—it can produce ugly objects as well as handsome ones in stultifying abundance. It serves only man's design. A machine can bulldoze green nature into the ugliest wasteland as easily as, in the hands of a good landscape architect, it can bring lovely greenery, a man-made lake, and even hills into a city. It can foul our air with stench and smog as easily as it can cool and heat it. It can ensnarl us in twice-daily traffic jams and never make up by transporting some of us at the speed of sound. It produces building materials of great efficiency and economy and helps us assemble them with astounding speed. But it can thereby also give us cities and suburbs of yawning, mass-produced monotony which further confounds our growing anxieties.

Frank Lloyd Wright was among the first to realize this paradox. He faced it with optimism. "In this day and generation," he prophesied in 1904, "we must recognize that this transforming force whose outward sign and symbol is the thing of brass and steel we call a machine, is now grown to the point that the artist must take it up, no longer to protest. Genius must dominate the work of the contrivance it has created. This plain duty is relentlessly marked out for the artist in this, the machine age. He cannot set it aside, although there is involved an adjustment to cherished gods, perplexing and painful in the extreme, and though the fires of long-honored ideals shall go down to ashes, they will reappear, phoenix-like, with new life and purpose."

Half a century earlier, in England, Ruskin and Morris had also sensed the danger. Their Arts and Crafts Movement attempted, however, to evade the machine. In the end, their handicrafts could no more hope to stem the tide of industrial production than an umbrella will protect you from atomic fall-out. It was necessary to reconcile art and industry. And this, in a somewhat vague and groping manner, is what an association of German craftsmen, artists and architects, called the *Werkbund,* set out to do. From the *Werkbund* emerged Walter Gropius, who, insulted by the chaos of the time, determined to "dominate the work of the contrivance." In 1919 he launched a school and laboratory of design which he called the Bauhaus, or house for building. Its declared intention was to absorb the spirit of engineering into art and the spirit of art into industrial design and architecture. He invited some of the greatest "fine" artists of our time to participate—among them Paul Klee, Wassily Kandinsky, Lyonel Feininger, Laszló Moholy-Nagy, and Josef Albers. Gropius' ultimate aim, as set forth in the first Bauhaus proclamation, was "to conceive and create the new building of the future, which will embrace architecture and sculpture and painting in one unity and which will rise one day toward heaven from the hands of a million workers like the crystal symbol of a new faith."

In time the phoenix did rise "with new life and purpose." And so did the crystal symbol. Frank Lloyd Wright—who with his Charnley house of 1891 was already more modern than the first stuttering motor cars of those days—gave architecture a new vocabulary of dynamic asymmetry, overlapping horizontal planes, and flowing interior spaces. His Prairie houses, built in the first decade of this century, contain an infinite number of innovations which, as Peter Blake has stated, still characterize the modern American residence: "Apart from the ribbon window and the corner window, Wright developed a window that was a casement opening out, rather than in; he began to plan his houses around a 'utility core'; he dramatized his rooms with 'cathedral ceilings'; he built concrete slab floors directly on the earth without basement, and set the radiant heating system into that floor. He designed an infinite variety of built-in furniture, including storage walls and built-in tables. He employed built-in lighting . . . and developed the 'carport' (beginning as the porte-cochère)."

Walter Gropius designed the building complex for his Bauhaus in Dessau, Germany, in 1922. It, too, turned out to be among the most remarkable and advanced structures of its period, and it still retains its freshness. Perhaps the most significant of its many ingenious features is the workshop building which is entirely sheathed in glass, in the "curtain wall" manner that Gropius had initiated with his Fagus shoe-last factory a decade earlier. In this building his instructors and students amalgamated and co-ordinated just about everything that was being tried in the arts and crafts of those days—Dada, constructivism, de Stijl, and all manner of expressionism—in virtually every medium from pottery to stagecraft. It thereby, in the words of Mies van der Rohe, who headed the Bauhaus from 1930 until the Nazis forced its closing in 1933, revolutionized our man-made environment "from the coffee cup to city planning."

Neither Wright nor Gropius stopped there. The Prairie houses were just a beginning of Wright's prolific creations, which gave us such varied and imaginative structures as his own home, Taliesin, in Wisconsin; "Falling Water"; the Johnson Wax building, and, in the end, the Guggenheim Museum in New York. Wright, however, always retained his touches of somewhat capricious, very personal Art Nouveau decorations. Gropius, in contrast, in his teaching and architecture, subjects all personal fancy to the aim of achieving unity and harmony in our environment. He strives for the synthesis of all demands and needs—human and technological—and he therefore advocates group work. Over a lifetime this design philosophy has carried him far from his early emphasis on the functional commodity of the Bauhaus to the unabashed delight of his not yet completed University of Baghdad.

Le Corbusier traveled even further. It was, as we said, a far stretch from his "machine-for-living-in" of the twenties to the exuberant sculpture of his chapel at Ronchamp or the forms and shapes at Chandigarh. Along the way he brought a profusion of ideas and innovations to our architecture. Among the more prosaic ones are the roof gardens and plazas on which children can play, and their parents enjoy the air and the view, far above the bustle of the street; the "pilotis" or stilts on which Corbu raises his buildings to make them appear both light and "muscular" and which permit free circulation beneath; the sun louvers or *brises-soleil* which keep the inside of a glass wall cool without reducing the light or view and which give the outside façade a pattern of light and shadow; and, finally, the on-the-site, fore-court plaza, achieved by setting a city building back on its allotted site to let both it and people gain from what has become the most precious urban luxury—open space. Corbu first used sun louvers and his set-back plaza, enlarged by the space under the stilts, on the Ministry of Education building in Rio de Janeiro, on which he collaborated in 1938 with Oscar Niemeyer, Lucio Costa, and other Brazilian architects. It has inspired a number of buildings in this book.

And so, to a far lesser extent as yet, has the poetry of Corbu's architecture; his search for ever-new shapes and forms and texture; "the search," to quote *Architectural Forum*, "for bold and simple forms, clearly man-made, raised up to be silhouetted against the sky; the search for tall, dramatic spaces of many levels that reflect the discovery of something new—the things that happen to a space as one moves through it; and the search for more plastic forms and spaces stimulated by new techniques in engineering."

But the most decisive influence on mid-century architecture in America was, undoubtedly, that of a master mason's son from Aachen, Germany—a man who never attended an architectural school. Compared to the opinionated loquacity and showmanship of Frank Lloyd Wright, Mies van der Rohe, who finds it painful to speak in public, seems a humble man indeed. Compared to the erudition of Gropius' philosophizing, Mies' rare pronouncements seem almost elementary. Compared to Corbu's temperamental, artistic *élan,* he seems but a workaday technician. Yet, Mies measures up to all of them in inspired self-assurance, in the depth and relevancy of his thinking, and in the creativeness of his art.

Mies seeks beauty in discipline, restraint, and the utmost refinements of the essentials of a building—its skin and bones. In his revolutionary skyscraper project of 1922, entirely enclosed in glass with its reflections, nothing but the interior columns which hold the floors like stacked trays make up the design. His Pavilion for the International Exposition at Barcelona in 1929 was another work of utter simplicity—an exercise in architectural composition. It contained none of the usual displays other than two water pools, lined in black glass, a statue by Georg Kolbe, and a most unusual proportioning of spaces opening into one another. It was built of such luxurious materials as travertine, marble, and chromium-plated steel columns and produced with much tender-loving refinement of detail. It is this refinement and the elegance of his proportions which make Mies' simple glass and steel boxes works of art.

His apartment towers built in 1951 on Lake Shore Drive in Chicago, for instance, are deceptively simple glass cages, window-walled on all sides and spaced to give each apartment the best possible view of Lake Michigan. But they do not appear as glass cages. Mies so designed the density of his eight-inch deep vertical mullions that they seem to overlap on the receding side of the building as you look at it. These mullions, in relation to the columns and bays, are of such classically perfect proportions that, as with the Parthenon, other architects find they must imitate them exactly or never emulate their effect.

Mies' unique achievement is that at a time when technology has made almost everything possible, he rejected most. He relies on creative thought in design, rather than originality, which is original enough. "Less is more," he has said. And he has thereby, in the view of his admirers, given his architecture a rare unity of commodity, firmness, and delight—of function, structure, and beauty.

If in this book more buildings will remind you of the work of Mies than of any of the other three great form-givers of our time, it is because as Arthur Drexler, the director of the Department of Architecture and Design of New York's Museum of Modern Art, has written, Mies' "ideas can be taught. His art is communicable. It can be practiced by others with measurable success." Or, as the *Architectural Record* put it: Thanks to Mies "some less able architects have been released from the imperatives of originality and architecture is the better for it."

Quite possibly it is. Whether or not, as Drexler says, Mies "is the architect par excellence of civilization, of law and order, of the great metropolis," the desperate need of our cities, our visual culture, *is* law and order. We want creativity, variety, and excitement to be sure. But do we not need unity and harmony even more? Much has been made in recent years of the uniformity and resultant monotony of entire streets and cities built in the "international style." It has been deplored along with an alleged increasing conformity in the ways of the American people. But those who criticize uniformity in the appearance of architecture today and at home often admire uniformity in the past and abroad.

Just recently an architect was praised for one of his buildings which is considerably below the surprisingly uniform cornice line of one of our few important avenues. This was hailed as "breaking up the canyon feeling of the street" and for being "in every way a departure" from neighboring structures. The same architect, at just about the same time recalled: "When I was in Copenhagen about twenty years ago, what struck me was the fact that the contemporary buildings were not all different. They were unified and created, in the city, a nice pleasant vista . . . quiet, fresh, and clean . . . very much like the people."

It has become fashionable to deplore the conformist but to send the maladjusted to the psychiatrist. Is it possible that man's overriding motive, urge, and *raison d'être* is survival and not self-realization; that conformity is not a bad thing at all? Is it conceivable that wanting to do as the Jonses do could be the natural, healthy, and normal way of living and surviving? Psychologists, who are largely responsible for this confusion, now seem to think so. They see survival dependent on the fact that individualistic drives are checked by the laws and order of the group. The tension generated by this interplay of the forces of individuality and creativity and the forces for conformity and for law and order are the mainspring of our inner life, the staff of our mental health. It is not one or the other which sustains the human spirit. Both are essential.

Perhaps it is now time for planners, architects, and their critics also to come around to this view—that unchecked individuality in architecture will ruin us as surely as monotony if it isn't subjected to order. We need the balance.

Conformity has never in itself been an evil. The beauty of Haussmann's boulevards in Paris is not due to original, or even particularly attractive, buildings. It was achieved by their conformity—by the discipline and restraint of their architects (and their clients) who, with the help of democratically adopted city regulations, subordinated them to a higher plan and ideal. Parisians, as they do now, cherished freedom of expression as much as we do. But they did not confuse it with bedlam—and now they cherish the beauty of their city even more. They know that the hand of the architect can still be distinct and personal, even if he writes identical words on uniformly ruled paper of standard size. Nor is the beauty of the Paris boulevards cold and monumental. As Lewis Mumford points out, they bustle with the lively human activity of their cafés—which were never on the drawing boards but which could fit into a larger order because that order was there in the first place.

It may well be, as some architects hold, that the answer is what Paul Rudolph has called "background" buildings—against which lively human activity and significant monuments, churches, and other important civic "foreground" structures stand out. The alternatives, says Peter Blake, "are architecture or Disneyland, civilization or chaos." Gropius and Mies seem to have created an appropriate idiom for much of "architecture," as opposed to "chaos." If that idiom has been called an "international style," what of it? Romanesque, Gothic, Renaissance, and Victorian also appeared in many countries and can thus also be called international styles. Yet, in each of these historic styles, individual genius and local culture, tradition, climate, and terrain were combined in some degree to produce their appropriate and necessary expression.

In attempting to sketch the origins and development of twentieth-century architecture, it is necessary to emphasize the contributions of four of its greatest masters. None of them originated it, however. Nor did they alone give it form and direction. The mainstream of our new architecture has many tributaries, most of them, as in all art, originating deep in history and fed by thousands of years of human culture.

The books of art historians who trace every likely or unlikely clue to discover who influenced whom—by what sketch or remark, at precisely what time—can be as entertaining as any detective mystery, but rarely as plausible. The world has become so small, and communication so rapid, that artist and architect cannot avoid constantly looking over each other's shoulder as they work. An idea sketched on the back of an envelope in São Paulo today may be published in millions of copies of a New York periodical tomorrow. The spoken word travels even faster. Who can honestly recall just whose sketch it was he saw in that magazine he thumbed through only this morning?

Suffice it, then, to say that out of numerous currents and cross-currents, out of new needs, out of new materials and engineering discoveries, and out of new concepts of beauty, a new architectural vocabulary emerged. And Frank Lloyd Wright, Walter Gropius, Le Corbusier and Mies van der Rohe have, to date, written its most impressive poems.

These are not included in this collection. It would have seemed supererogatory, somehow, for these masters, who were all four honored with the Gold Medal of AIA, to submit their work to its juries, although the Americans Wright, Mies, and Gropius were, of course, technically entitled to do so.

Nor is there a building depicted on these pages which does not in one way or another, consciously or subconsciously, reveal the impact of their contribution.

The debt to European genius, to be sure, is great, but the European avant-garde, in turn, readily acknowledges its debt to us. In culture and technology, the Atlantic Community—the interchange of ideas and ideals between Europe and America—existed long before now. Henry Luce, however, I am sure, did not have the influence of Jenny or Louis Sullivan (to say nothing of those well-photographed Midwestern grain elevators) in mind, when he claimed that the architectural revolution was accomplished mainly in America. Nor did he think only of Frank Lloyd Wright, for the American counted far more in Europe than he did in his own country until, as John Burchard and Albert Bush-Brown state, it "developed a modern architecture by assimilating yet another immigrant art form and gradually modifying it to its characteristic institutions and thereby making it as American as any architecture was likely ever to be."

"Modifying" seems too weak a word. For, to quote Burchard and Bush-Brown again, "the art was not so pure when it arrived; it was nothing like what Wright would have it." Or the Frenchman, Corbu. Or the Finn, Alvar Aalto. Or the Austrian turned American, Richard Neutra. Or the Germans, Gropius and Mies, who became citizens of this country when Hitler turned their homeland into a death camp for the free, creative spirit. It was from Harvard that Gropius, and from the Illinois Institute of Technology that Mies, with their students and with challenging new commissions, created a language of their vocabulary. None of the European avant-garde had actually built much more than a handful of structures—experiments, in a sense, declarations of a new faith. They had more on paper, particularly Corbu, and much of it remains prophetic to this day. But the new technology and the new way of life these declarations called for were not fully realized until they found their echo in America.

As World War II threatened, their ideas still were not fully realized. Buckminster Fuller complained at about that time, and not without justice, that the new architecture "used standard plumbing fixtures and only ventured so far as to persuade manufacturers to modify the surface of the valve handles and spigots, and the color, size and arrangements of the tiles. . . . [It] never went back of the wall-surface to look at the plumbing . . . in short [it] only looked at problems of modification of the surface of end-products, which end-products were inherently sub-functions of a technically obsolete world."

Two decades later our engineers and manufacturers are still far from the dymaxion world of Fuller. But we have developed and mass-produced miracles of ingenuity and efficiency too numerous to name. It was such innovations as new curtain-wall materials, glare- and heat-resistant glass, automatic elevators, heating and air conditioning systems, and a host of other technical innovations and improvements which gave meaning to the new architecture.

And so did a new way of life. Postwar America called for new types of buildings, which, in turn, helped to mold its pattern. The modern motel is one example. Another is the suburban shopping center. Atomic reactor stations are entirely postwar building types. Much has been said and written about the rapid transformation of our society—its newly shared wealth, the release from manual drudgery, a house for every family, and mass transportation, mass communication, and mass culture. All this is reflected by our architecture, and our architecture at the same time molds and shapes it all.

Buildings both reflect and determine a civilization. For better or for worse, American civilization is now changing the world. And along with Coca-Cola, jazz, and (hopefully) our concepts of constitutional democracy, our architects are busy on all continents exporting our architecture. We did not invent that architecture alone. Neither did we invent *egalité, fraternité* and *liberté*. We did, however, build these concepts into a viable, dynamic system.

We need not become chauvinistic about this. Our debt to Europe, as we shall see, continues. Latin America is now influencing our architecture as, earlier, did Japan. Also, while it did happen here in the end, the American people have accepted the new architecture only slowly and with less than unanimous enthusiasm. In contrast to the princes and archbishops of the middle ages and Renaissance who took no chances with the individual tastes and inclinations of the people, democracy poses considerable problems for those who attempt to reflect it visually. As Gropius put it recently, "the architect and artist of the twentieth century has to face a completely new client and patron: the average citizen or his representative whose stature, opinion and influence are uncertain and difficult to define compared to the authoritarian lord of the past. . . . This citizen, as of now, is not at all in the habit of extending his vision beyond his immediate business concerns because we have neglected to educate him for his role of cultural arbiter. He repays his neglect by running loose, only here and there restricted by social ambitions from recklessly following his commercial interests. Though he is quite aware of the restrictions the law puts on his building activities, he is almost totally unaware of his potentialities to contribute something positive, socially and culturally, to the actual development, change and improvement of his environment."

As late as 1958, some congressmen deplored Skidmore, Owings and Merrill's striking design of the Air Force Academy Chapel as "an insult to the Almighty." And even today a majority seems to believe that only shrunken colonial, Cape Cod ranches, or Cinderella homes properly represent the American way of life. At least that is what a good many home builders seem to think. However, a trend has now begun working the other way. For it is slowly becoming apparent to people that architects working with builders can give them better, more thoughtful design for their money.

Yet, even those who still prefer "traditional" at home accept "modern" as the appropriate architecture for the schools of their children, their places of business, and—a little more reluctantly—for their churches and temples.

No sooner has America embraced the new architecture than it has blossomed out into a richness and inventiveness that must, in retrospect, astound even its most daring prophets. Its stark, bare, and square austerity, largely a gesture of protest against over-decorative eclecticism, has given way to a less self-conscious expression.

Taking up the fundamental tenets of the earlier "modern," a new modified modern with three basic characteristics has developed. These characteristics are:

First, a totally new emphasis on the interior spaces of a building in terms of their usefulness, comfort, and beauty and their inter-relationship. In the past, rooms within a building were rigid compartments. Interior spaces are more flexible and sometimes can be divided at will. They open and flow into one another in a dynamic rather than static relationship.

Second, there is a new indoor-outdoor relationship. The use (some complain the overuse) of glass has made it possible to bring nature's plants and greenery into the building, and extend the building out into nature. Planted plazas, interior courts, and terraces have brought nature even into our urban working environment.

Third, our buildings appear lighter, often buoyant. Skyscrapers soar effortlessly into the air. Other buildings rest lightly on the ground as though to disturb it as little as possible. Even where they hug the earth and adapt to its contours, they avoid being massive and ponderous.

If one word were to summarize the aspiration of American architecture at mid-century, that word would be "liveability." It first appeared early in the fifties, and it indicates a new concern with the amenities and aesthetics of comfortable living and working conditions in all types of buildings. Residences, schools, hospitals, office, industrial, and commercial buildings and our religious, civic, and cultural centers are designed with a new emphasis on "human scale," with the intent to meet man's emotional and spiritual needs as well as his physical ones.

The all-too-few architect-designed houses of the fifties reflect a striving for privacy, for an intensification of the inner life, and for a communion with nature. "Togetherness" and its "open plan," on which the entire family camps in unhappy confusion, constituted, it appears, a passing fad which enthused the editors of some magazines far more than their readers.

All the award-winning houses share an emphatic withdrawal from the bustle of the street and from ostentation as well. Gone are the front yards which serve no purpose but to keep the lawnmowers humming in tribute to the good old days of Georgian country manors. As usable space within reasonable commuting distances becomes increasingly one of our most precious commodities, the zoning and building code requirements for setbacks have become a wasteful anachronism. As some of the residences in this book and most Mediterranean towns prove, the appearance of a street need not suffer if its houses turn their backs to it. Placing the house on the street side of the lot gains the owner much useful space and adds seclusion and security.

The interior, too, emphasizes privacy for the members of the family from each other. The children's right to their noisy pursuits is recognized along with that of their parents *not* to hear Huckleberry Hound's televised antics. Indoors and outdoors merge, as we said, with actual and visual openings into patios and sheltered terraces. Even where actual space is limited, built-in furnishings, glass walls, and a flowing openness towards the sheltered patio combine to give the house a feeling of spaciousness.

The new emphasis on the garden and the natural setting brought with it a new emphasis on the orientation of the house. Robert Anshen has reminded us again of Socrates' wisdom. The philosopher asked: "Should a house be a pleasant place to live in and a safe place to store one's belongings?" When his listeners agreed he asked further: "Well, then, should a house be cool in the summer and warm in the winter?" When, again, they nodded agreement, he declared: "If you build the north side low and the porticos high and facing south, the building will be protected from the cold in the winter and, in the summer when the sun is high, it will cast shade and it will be cool, but in the winter, when the sun is low, warm. If, then, these are desirable characteristics, this is the way to build a house."

Careful orientation also makes the most of existing trees, rocks, and the topography. The design of the garden becomes as important as that of the living room, which, in a sense, it becomes—a place inviting quiet meditation.

School buildings, rather than being places to confine children for the ordeal of getting an education, have themselves become tools of teaching. Leading among the first truly contemporary school buildings was the Crow Island School, at Winnetka, Illinois, built in 1940 by Perkins and Will in association with Eliel Saarinen. It helped set the pattern for what followed. A spreading, one-story building, it was by no means luxurious, using a common brick normally relegated to the back of inexpensive apartment houses. Yet its light, cheerful appearance of spaciousness gives it elegance and delight along with commodity. Different age groups are separated in four wings, each with its outdoor play area. The classroom units are L-shaped with a work area in the short side and the classroom itself in the long side. The space and the movable furniture permit informal grouping, and the orientation makes the most of natural light. Each classroom unit lets the children directly out into the open (important in case of fire), and its generous windows include the world beyond.

Whether arranged in a finger plan or cluster, all the schools shown in these pages follow this principle of controlled openness to their lovingly landscaped setting. Ingenious use of materials, contrast, and color are applied to making the place of learning cheerful and attractive as well as functional. Some of these schools even venture into a judicious and economical use of art work.

It thus came to pass, as Burchard and Bush-Brown put it, "that the finest living and aesthetic experience in the life of many American children came to them in their schools. . . . There seemed little doubt that America led the world in this kind of architecture." What accounts for this success is, according to Lawrence B. Perkins, more than technology, "the changing awareness of how people use buildings, how they feel about buildings, how learning takes place."

Yet for all their winning appearance and the recurring attacks on them for alleged "frills" and waste, school buildings today are the best buy on the building market. Conscious of the taxpayers' predicament, architects have succeeded in keeping construction and maintenance cost of schools amazingly low. While the cost of all building has tripled during the past twenty years, the cost of school building has, on the average, doubled during that period.

A similar development has taken place in hospital design. The earlier tendency was to incorporate into spotless health factories all the advances in medical knowledge and technology with the greatest possible efficiency and aseptic polish. In the fifties our hospitals and clinical facilities took efficiency for granted and, again, concentrated on liveability, on charm and cheer as an indispensable psychological incentive to healing and convalescence.

While office buildings generally followed the already discussed Miesian formula of curtain-wall design, some notable commercial, civic, and cultural centers, and particularly churches, were affected by yet another fundamental technological development. Completely new forms and shapes and the spanning of large spaces without columns or other interior obstructions have been made possible by a major breakthrough from the age-old structure of compressive strength to a new structure of tension.

Again the debt to European genius is great. Based on intricate mathematical calculations of stress and tension, engineering pioneers like the Italian, Pier Luigi Nervi, and the Spaniard, Eduardo Torroja, have broken the tyranny of cubical forms by developing what might be called shell construction. In this method, walls and roof, support and load, framework and ornament are one as in the egg, a form nature often uses to protect life at its most vulnerable beginning. Other shapes which derive their strength from form rather than mass are the saddle-back hyperbolic paraboloid and crimped triangles which stand up as even this paper will if you fold it repeatedly.

With such new structural forms, reinforced concrete—only recently rediscovered in steel-rich America—came fully into its own. The Romans had already used concrete, which can be shaped and sculptured like "molten stone," as Nervi said. But thin, flexible skins are possible only when it is re-inforced with steel wires. "Steel," writes Torroja, "gives tenacity to stone. Concrete gives mass to steel. Combined they will resist tension in accordance with the existing network of stresses" to reach out and span space of fantastic proportions. But free forms, the architecture of tension, are possible in other materials as well. Buckminster Fuller employs the principle with his geodesic constructions in steel, aluminum, and plastics. Mathematics and engineering have here once more given the architect new, almost unlimited structural and sculptural possibilities—as well as new responsibilities. For, again, mere possibility must be subjected to art and its dictates of beauty and appropriateness.

To build a church or temple, in an age when any billboard can dwarf the steeple and any loudspeaker can drown out the bells, is indeed, as the Archbishop of Besançon said when he dedicated Le Corbusier's chapel at Ronchamp, "an act of optimism." With an unprecedented need for new religious centers, hundreds of architects have recently committed such an act. They have given us, as the Reverend George Miles Gibson, of McCormick Theological Seminary suggests, "new sermons in stone, steel and glass."

The challenge of designing a place to worship is greater than any other. There are the complex functional needs of the church or synagogue: the need to accommodate large congregations on important holidays without making the much smaller number of faithful on ordinary Sundays feel lost; the need to accommodate meaningful liturgy and tradition without clinging to meaningless conventions; the need to express the religious outlook of the congregation which may desire withdrawal or world-openness. There is also the vague but insistent demand of some congregations that "a church look like a church." And within it, the architect must create a quality of space which, as the late architectural writer John Knox Shear has said, "has something there, that wasn't put there."

Not all problems of church architecture have been solved. Too many architects still shrink from honest statements. They strive to "adjust" to the suburban environment for which a roadside chain restaurant in "Turnpike Colonial" seems to have set the architectural style. Within their sanctuaries, architects often artificially create a religious "mood" with their planter arrangements and with theatrical lighting controlled by push-buttons from the pulpit.

But there is also a surprising number of architects who have successfully met the challenge. Their materials, construction methods, and forms vary almost from building to building. We see the divergent influences of Frank Lloyd Wright (particularly his folded roof structure, "the praying hands," of the Madison, Wisconsin, Unitarian Church,) of Le Corbusier and his sculptured concrete forms, and more often of Eliel Saarinen's movingly simple Christ Lutheran Church at Minneapolis, built in 1949. Yet, despite this variety, greater than in any other building type, there seems to emerge a unity of expression which is not yet a "style."

If our architecture expresses the spirit of our times, our best churches and temples, our best houses, offices, schools, and other buildings, give cause for optimism—certainly more cause than do the other arts.

The moment in history of many of the buildings shown here has been called "the fearful 'fifties." It is a time in which most painters and sculptors still persisted in their disdain of humanism, retreating into uncommunicative, abstract confusion. The excuse is not hard to find. In our country this period began, it will be recalled, with headlines about the Berlin airlift and the Korean War, with McCarthyism and gaudy Senate hearings. It also began with the illusion that these United States had a monopoly on nuclear weapons and, perhaps, even on virtue. *Newsweek* proclaimed early in the 'fifties, "It is no wonder that . . . many consider the U. S. a land in which the Spirit—that refugee from most parts of the modern world—has made His home." Most of us sang "Goodnight Irene," thrilled to the eerie tune of "The Third Man Theme," read Gayelord Hauser's *Look Younger, Live Longer,* and launched an ever-mounting building boom by escaping to a picture window of our own in the suburbs.

A few of us, with John Keats, soon suspected *The Crack in the Picture Window* and worried with David Riesman about *The Lonely Crowd.* We preferred to read Hemingway's bitter *Across the River and Into the Trees* and Budd Schulberg's *The Disenchanted.* We admired Jackson Pollock and William de Kooning's rather savage and pessimistic art.

As America moved into the 'sixties the headlines were as black as ever with crises abroad and in our own South. The illusion of virtue had vanished as did our atomic monopoly. Our faith in America's absolute technological superiority was shattered as satellites followed sputniks and Commander Shepard followed Major Gagarin into outer space. What with television scandals and organization men convicted of price fixing, *Newsweek,* as Meg Greenfield observed in *The Reporter,* now wondered if "our culture . . . is going rancid." We considered ourselves, at any rate, not just rich, but an "affluent" society with, as John Kenneth Galbraith complained, "no highly developed sense of national purpose, with the overwhelming accent of life on personal comfort, with a dearth of public services and a surfeit of privately sold gadgetry, and with insufficient social discipline." The music writer of the *Encyclopaedia Britannica Yearbook* gave up naming the titles of the hit songs—mostly rock'n'roll—which filled the airwaves as "worthless trash." The bestseller was *Peyton Place.*

Yet, there was also a growing number of us who read *Exodus* and *Doctor Zhivago,* who mourned the untimely death of Albert Camus, and who accounted for the phenomenal output of classical records and good paperback books. This minority thought that the popular "tide of moral revulsion," was perhaps a healthy sign. It saw a significance in the fact that, in contrast to his predecessor, who reportedly flushed with anger over the modern design of a public building, the new President invited leading modern architects, along with other artists and "egg-heads," to his inauguration.

If architects shared these fluctuating emotions of uncertainty about our culture and its values, their architecture certainly did not. It continues in what critic Ada Louise Huxtable has termed "a singular state of vital and positive productivity." It was, if anything, more optimistic than ever before in our history, tending, in fact, towards buoyant romanticism. Some even saw a "modern baroque" in such buildings as Edward D. Stone's "pill factory," the Stuart Pharmaceutical Company Headquarters, and Minoru Yamasaki's Community Center on the Wayne University campus and his Reynolds Metals Company building in Detroit. Baroque or not, these and a good many other buildings dared a decorativeness which rivals that of the Alhambra and Venetian Gothic.

In their earlier, self-conscious and defensive stage, modern architects tended to insist they were mere technicians of function, just good old Yankee businessmen, who used their newfangled modernism only because it gave you the most shelter for your money. They "satisfied function, not fashion," they said. They still do. But they now realize, in Giedion's words, that "people want the buildings that represent their social and community life to give more than functional fulfillment. They want their aspirations for monumentality, joy, pride and excitement to be satisfied."

Ed Stone was among the first to exclaim: "Let's go to bat for beauty!" Yamasaki holds that beauty is a need in life which architecture must satisfy by being an object of love. "Our democratic ideals," he said, "need buildings that give us, instead of a sense of awe, a sense of happiness, peace, security." Other architects agree. They now cheerfully acknowledge that in addition to being expert technicians, mindful of their client's needs and pocketbook, they are also artists—and proud of it. And—as sculptor Richard Lippold has stated—"the truly creative man has faith in his time."

How well American architecture's faith in our time, its new burst of creativity, succeeds in pleasing us and posterity, only we and posterity can tell. May both remember, however, as Nervi stated, "that all the qualities of a people and of a period are concentrated and, as it were, fossilized in its architecture. For everyone contributes to architecture: the client, with the exact definition of his requirements and with the choice of designer; the architect in the function of interpreter or rather catalyst, of the deep and sometimes unconscious feelings of the society in which he lives; the general public, which judges a work of architecture with the immediacy which comes from the very fact of living in it or beside it and, by its verdict, influences succeeding developments in building."

The profession of architecture, at any rate, is far from satisfied. "I think I feel before me a very troubled and very disturbed profession," architect Philip Will, Jr. told his colleagues upon his election to the presidency of the AIA in 1960. This concern is not confined solely to the enormous problem of keeping abreast of the growing complexity of technological advances and of changing social and economic demands on the individual building; it is also a deep concern over the ever more apparent ugliness, confusion, and inefficiency of urban America. The city, as Mumford, has said, "has been disappearing before our eyes, sinking under a tidal wave of motor cars and parking lots . . . being thinned out into a suburban conglomeration." Isolated handsome buildings cannot save it until they add up to handsome streets, squares, and neighborhoods. And in adding them, liveability must now be extended to the whole of urban design.

The task is not for architects alone. It requires the total mobilization not only of our scientific, social, economic, and political skills but also (and especially) of our popular will to bring order into our cities and suburbs. Only order can make beauty possible.

It would seem that the twentieth-century revolution in architecture has given us the kind of buildings which hold that promise. We have a new architecture. Now it must meet our demands for a liveable and attractive environment. "Certainly," as Mies has said, "it is not necessary or possible to invent a new kind of architecture every Monday morning."

THE AIA "HONOR AWARDS FOR CURRENT WORK" AND ITS JURIES

Edmund R. Purves, FAIA, Consulting Director

AS AN ORGANIZATION which since its inception has been engaged in advancing the architectural profession's objective to serve society, The American Institute of Architects undertook not only to encourage actively the perfection of the product of its members but also to obtain public recognition and acclaim for that product. This is why the Honor Awards for Current Work program came into being in 1949. The Institute for many years had been engrossed in the difficult and often frustrating task of establishing the profession and itself on a firm footing; and now, that having been accomplished, it was able to turn to the more delightful and fascinating aspects of its concerns.

In 1948, at the convention held in Grand Rapids, Michigan, a resolution was adopted which called for the establishment of a committee to bring before the Institute a concrete proposal for an honor awards program for current work. The then President of the Institute, Douglas Orr, thereupon appointed the late Albert Frederic Heino of Chicago as chairman of the committee. Al Heino was a dedicated worker in the welfare of the Institute and continually strove to gain appropriate recognition for his colleagues by the public.

In December, 1948, Heino presented his program to the Board of Directors at its meeting at Sea Island, Georgia. His recommendations were instantly and enthusiastically adopted. As is the fate of all good workers who have been entrusted with the formulation of a plan for a project, the project itself was delegated to the proposer. So Heino found himself appointed Chairman of the Committee on Honor Awards Program.

It was a task of no small proportions. He had to explain; to instill enthusiasm; and to ensure the success of his first venture. For several years the magazine *Progressive Architecture* had been conducting its own honor award program. To avoid confusion, that magazine graciously discontinued its effort and supported the Institute's program in order that there might be only one honor awards program. The Institute has been grateful to *Progressive Architecture* ever since for its generous action.

In its first years, the AIA program was somewhat experimental in nature, and several conditions were imposed at the outset which were discontinued in time. For instance, at first it was decided to restrict entrants to corporate members of the Institute. In a year or so this restriction was rescinded, and it became quite obvious that when an organization selects the outstanding work of the year, that entry should be open to everyone legally entitled to call himself an architect.

For two or three years the program was run on a category basis, and each year the Executive Committee or the Board would select, upon the recommendation of the Committee, those categories which were to be featured at the coming convention. The categories were in building types: schools, churches, hospitals, residences, commercial buildings, and so on. But this restriction by categories proved to be quite unsatisfactory. The categories were poorly balanced one with another, and there were one or two rather sad occasions when the category failed to achieve a single mention. Unexpectedly the use of categories became a rather invidious restriction, so now the Honor Awards Program is a simple matter of straightforward awards.

Of course, the Honor Awards Program met with some opposition, as there is always someone who will oppose an idea. But the program survived, and now we have at our annual conventions, thanks to the foresight of the Institute, and particularly to the dedication of the late Al Heino, an architectural exhibit which has become of increasing importance and which is already recognized as a major affair in architectural circles.

That this is so is, of course, largely due to the high caliber of the juries. The illustrious list of their names speaks for itself. Members of the jury were:

1949:

Mrs. Katherine Morrow Ford
Karl Kamrath, AIA
Kenneth Stowell, AIA
John Dinwiddie, AIA
Walter F. Bogner, AIA, Chairman

1950:

For Commercial Architecture

Walter O. Bode
Kenneth C. Welch, AIA
James A. Wares, AIA
Harold D. Hauf, AIA
Lawrence B. Anderson, AIA

For Residential Design

Elizabeth Gordon
Pietro Belluschi, FAIA
Thomas H. Creighton, AIA
George M. Martin, FAIA
James T. Lendrum, AIA

For Ecclesiastical Architecture

William Ward Watkin, FAIA
Ernest A. Grunsfeld, Jr., FAIA
Charles I. Baker, AIA
Thomas H. Locraft, AIA
Maurice Lavanoux

1951:

Hospital Classification

Dr. Herman Smith
Perry B. Johanson, AIA
Harold Bush-Brown, FAIA
Harrison Gill, AIA
Addison Erdman, AIA

Industrial Classification

Fred L. Markham, AIA
Carter E. Hewitt, AIA
C. Theodore Larson, AIA
Joseph Z. Burger
Dale Purves

Residential Classification

Cloethiel Woodward Smith, AIA
Mrs. Florence Byerly
Paul Schweikher, AIA
Abraham W. Geller, AIA
Milton S. Osborne, AIA

1952:

James A. Mitchell, AIA
Samuel E. Lunden, FAIA
Joseph D. Murphy, AIA
Glenn Stanton, FAIA
O. J. Teegen, AIA

1953:

Lawrence G. Waldron, AIA, Chairman
Arthur P. Herman, FAIA
Rollin H. Boles, AIA
H. Abbott Lawrence, AIA
Charles H. Gordon
Frederick M. Hunter
Walter L. Doty
F. O. Stringfellow

1954:

Hugh A. Stubbins, Jr., AIA, Chairman
Robert T. Coolidge
Robert A. Jacobs, FAIA
Harold R. Sleeper, FAIA
Richard L. Howland, AIA
Donald Rosenberger
Barbara Wriston

1955:

Thomas H. Locraft, FAIA, Chairman
Ernest Born, FAIA
Eugene F. Kennedy, FAIA
Ludwig Mies van der Rohe, FAIA
J. Byers Hays, FAIA

1956:

Eero Saarinen, FAIA, Chairman
Pietro Belluschi, FAIA
George B. Allison, FAIA
Donald S. Nelson, FAIA
Paul Thiry, FAIA

1957:

Roy F. Larson, FAIA, Chairman
John Knox Shear, AIA
James M. Hunter, FAIA
Philip D. Creer, FAIA
Alden B. Dow, FAIA

1958:

Jean Labatut, AIA, Chairman
Igor B. Polevitzky, FAIA
Frederick James MacKie, FAIA
John Gaw Meem, FAIA
Welton Becket, FAIA

1959:

Walter Bogner, FAIA, Chairman
Walter Gordon, AIA
Albert S. Golemon, FAIA
Vincent G. Kling, AIA
Harry Weese, AIA

1960:

G. Holmes Perkins, FAIA, Chairman
Alfred Shaw, FAIA
Harris Armstrong, FAIA
Alfred L. Aydelott, AIA
Henry L. Kamphoefner, FAIA

1961:

Morris Ketchum, Jr., FAIA, Chairman
Fred Bassetti, AIA
Richard D. Butterfield, FAIA
Arthur Q. Davis, FAIA
William L. Pereira, FAIA

Works granted Awards of Merit are dated in the text from the year of their completion, and not according to the year in which the Award was conferred.

MID-CENTURY ARCHITECTURE IN AMERICA

1166609

1

OFFICE BUILDINGS

Skidmore, Owings & Merrill

Lever House, New York City. 1952 Honor Award. Owner: Lever Brothers.

Photos: (exterior) J. Alex Langley, (interior) Ezra Stoller.

Le Corbusier, with the Ministry of Education Building in Rio de Janeiro (1937 to 1943) supplied the inspiration for the thin stilted slab with its low connecting wing, which offers an exciting contrast in scale, and for raising the building so that it is no longer a barrier to pedestrian circulation. Instead, it opens invitingly to its interior court. Mies van der Rohe inspired the crystalline clarity of the design which openly expresses its structure and plan. The result is this famous structure, which, perhaps more than any other, set a pattern for mid-century city architecture in America. Its most important innovation is not the spirited, wavering sheen of the stainless steel and green glass façade, but its disciplined restraint: Lever House uses only one-quarter of its lot. It opens up downtown congestion, provides breathing space and greenery, as well as a high degree of interior amenity. None of the office desks is more than 25 feet from a window wall, which provides carefully controlled daylight and a view.

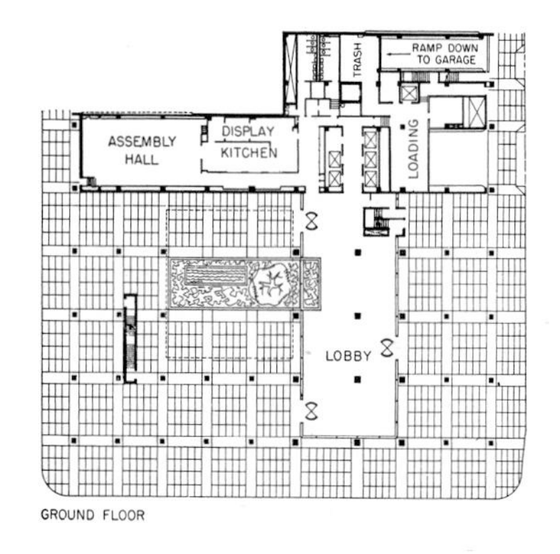

GROUND FLOOR

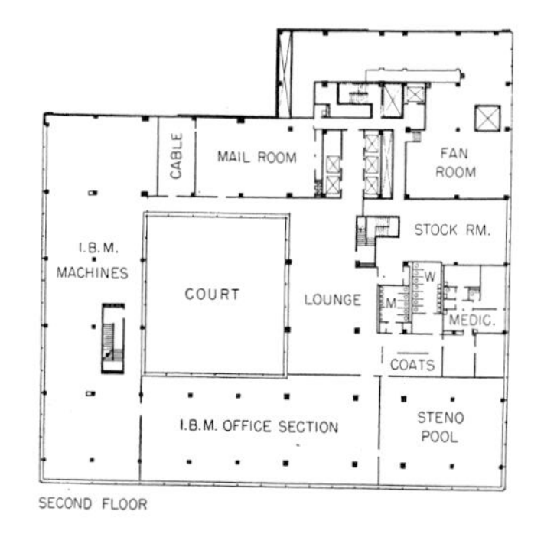

SECOND FLOOR

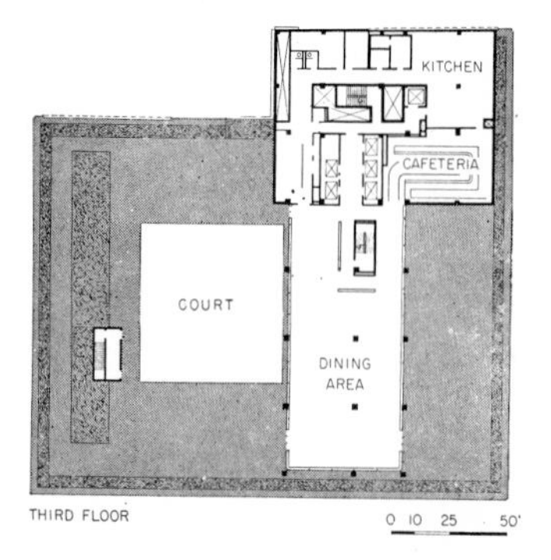

THIRD FLOOR

William S. Beckett

William S. Beckett's Office, Los Angeles, California. 1952 Honor Award.

Photos: Julius Shulman.

In designing his own office, the architect has here carried the Miesian idiom to a highly decorative statement. Within a basic rectangular form he defined both exterior and interior spaces by cabinets, hanging walls, hardwood panels, sheets of glass, and sheets of metal. The major interior volume of the building forms the drafting room which, opens through sliding glass doors to a garden as well as to the private office. A gallery, accessible from the drafting room, extends above the conference and reception rooms.

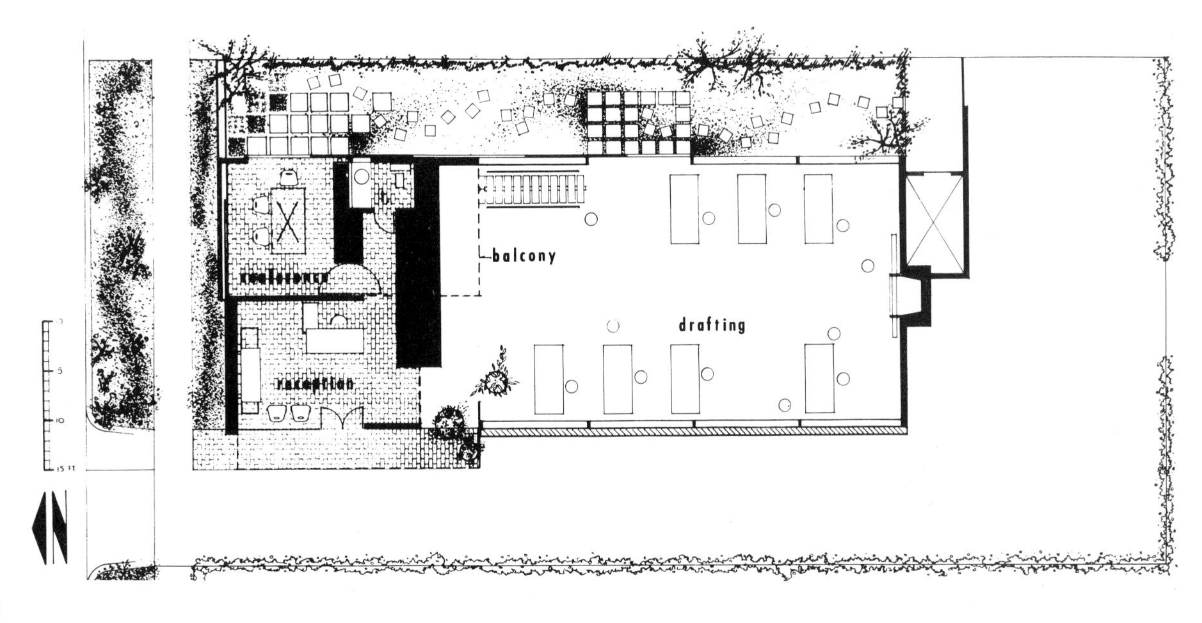
balcony
drafting
5
10
15 FT

Richard J. Neutra

Insurance Office Building, Los Angeles, California. 1951. Owner: Northwestern Mutual Insurance Co. Photo: Julius Shulman.

Pereira & Luckman

CBS Television City, Los Angeles, California. 1952. Owner: Columbia Broadcasting System, Inc. Photo: Julius Shulman.

Welton Becket and Associates

Standard Federal Savings & Loan Association, Los Angeles, California. 1953. Owner: California Federal Savings & Loan Association. Photo: Douglas M. Simmonds.

Killingsworth, Brady and Smith

Architects' Office, Long Beach, California. 1955. Photo: Marvin Rand.

Philip C. Johnson

Schlumberger Administration Building, Ridgefield, Connecticut. 1952. Owner: Schlumberger Well Surveying Co. Photo: Ben Schnall.

Anderson, Beckwith and Haible

Middlesex Mutual Building Trust, Waltham, Massachusetts. 1957 Honor Award.

Photos: Louis Reens.

This office building in an attractive rural setting is designed for two insurance companies with a single management and certain common departments. The landscaped court evolved naturally from the aim to tie them together and provide easy access to the joint services; to get light into the interior; and to provide a focal point for the surrounding activities. The cafeteria and lounge were placed on the penthouse, which affords a magnificent view. They are reached from the interior by a wide ramp (more pleasant to walk than a crowded staircase) and from the court by stairs which lead to an adjoining terrace.

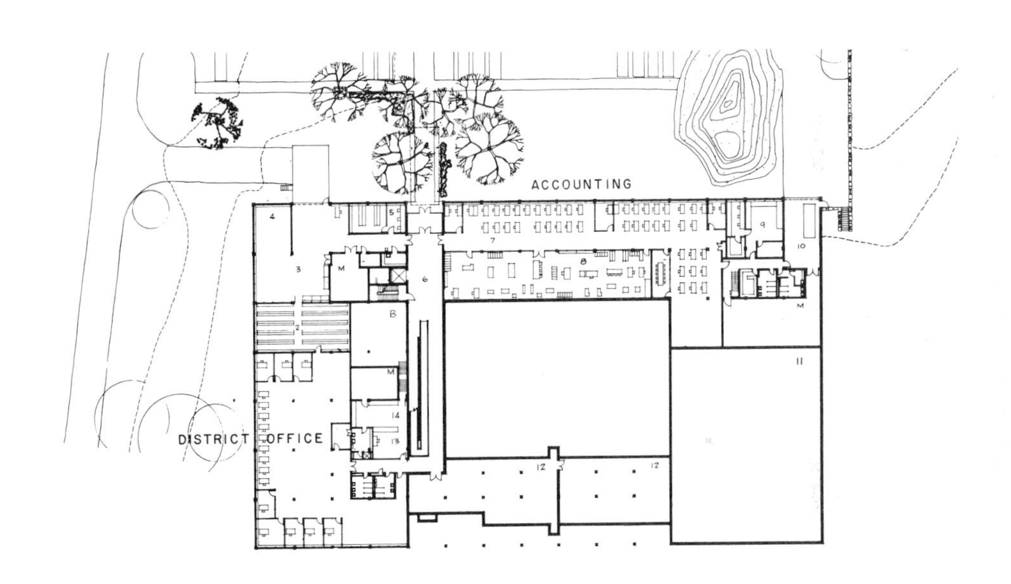

Skidmore, Owings & Merrill

Connecticut General Life Insurance Company, Bloomfield, Connecticut.

1958 Honor Award. Photos: Ezra Stoller.

One can make light of the modern corporation's "crystal palace" with its seductive comforts for "the organization man." But the fact remains that the girls dress up to do their clerical chores in this building. Their pride in the stylish surroundings—which include garden courts, art works, a theater, bowling alleys, tennis courts, a shop, an attractive cafeteria, not to speak of ample and meticulously planned work space—reduces personnel turnover. Amenity increases efficiency. The architects managed to break up the hugeness of the building by opening it up to an ever-changing variety of courts and interior spaces beyond which one never loses awareness of the pastoral Connecticut landscape.

I. M. Pei & Associates

Zeckendorf Plaza Development: May-D&F Department Store and Denver Hilton Hotel.
Photos: Warren Reynolds and Guy Burgess.

New York's Rockefeller Center, built in the early nineteen-thirties, demonstrated a new approach to urban planning: a handsome sequence of masses and spaces which provide greenery, variety, and interest to pedestrians. Zeckendorf Plaza follows this pattern. It is comprised of three buildings in the heart of downtown Denver, each different in scale, materials, and façade treatment, and each carefully related to the other in a cluster, making room for a tree-shaded plaza and a sunken skating rink. The department store (1959 Honor Award) brings the amenities of suburban shopping —convenient parking, one-stop shopping, and an inviting atmosphere of open space— back into the city. The adjoining hyperbolic paraboloid shell pavilion contains a store and the main entrance. The 21-story hotel (1961 Award of Merit) with its luxurious interiors and art works emphasizes elegance both inside and out. It is connected with the department store by a bridge enclosed in clear plastic and shares its underground, three-level parking garage.

Kenneth W. Brooks, Bruce M. Walker

Central Service Facility, Spokane, Washington. 1959 Honor Award.

Owner: Washington Water Power Company. Photos: Morley Baer.

This sizeable project was the first major commission of two young architects who teamed up for the job. Its purpose is to consolidate a variety of shops, warehouses, storage yards, and offices previously scattered over thirteen different locations. The result is a complete and harmoniously unified complex which includes all of the Water Power Company's facilities from the 40-ton crane to the last filing cabinet. The handsome structures in the Miesian vein and the careful landscaping combine to enhance the Spokane River waterfront.

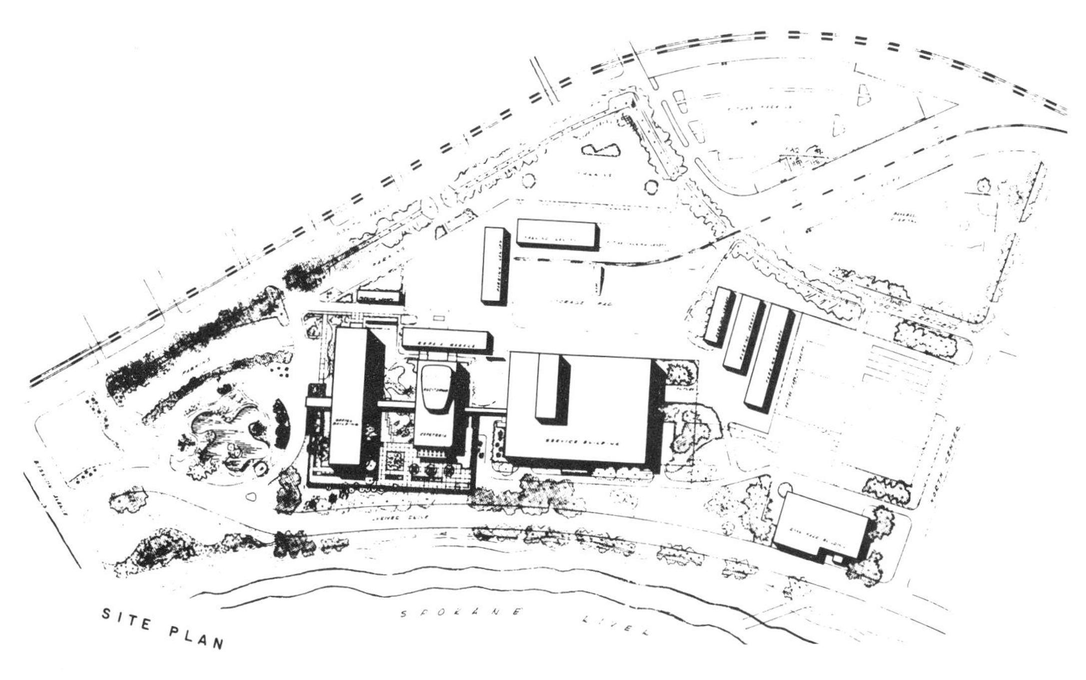

SITE PLAN

Golemon & Rolfe

The Medical Towers, Houston, Texas. 1956. Owner: Center Land Company. Photo: Harper Lieper.

I. M. Pei & Associates
Kahn & Jacobs, Associate Architects

Mile High Center, Denver, Colorado. 1955. Owner: Webb & Knapp, Inc., N. Y. and George A. Fuller Co., N. Y. Photo: Ezra Stoller.

Perkins & Will

International Minerals & Chemical Corporation, Administrative and Research Center, Skokie, Illinois. 1958. Photo: Hedrich-Blessing.

Hertzka & Knowles
Skidmore, Owings & Merrill, Associate Architects

Crown Zellerbach Building, San Francisco, California. 1959. Owner: New York Life Insurance Company. Photo: Morley Baer.

Killingsworth, Brady, Smith and Associates

Office Building for a Development Firm, Long Beach, California. 1960. Owner: Cambridge Investments. Photo: Marvin Rand.

Sherwood, Mills and Smith

Mutual Insurance Company of Hartford, Hartford, Connecticut.

1960 Honor Award. Photos: Robert Stahman.

Here a simple steel-frame construction gains its significance by the use of art—a lively yet pleasingly harmonious mural relief designed and cast by sculptor Constantino Nivola. The jury highly commended this successful and all too rare integration of art and architecture. The relief is on the east wall which, like the west wall, consists of precast concrete panels bolted to the steel frame. Aluminum and heat-absorbing glass curtain walls on the north and south side of the building provide light and a view onto the well-landscaped surroundings.

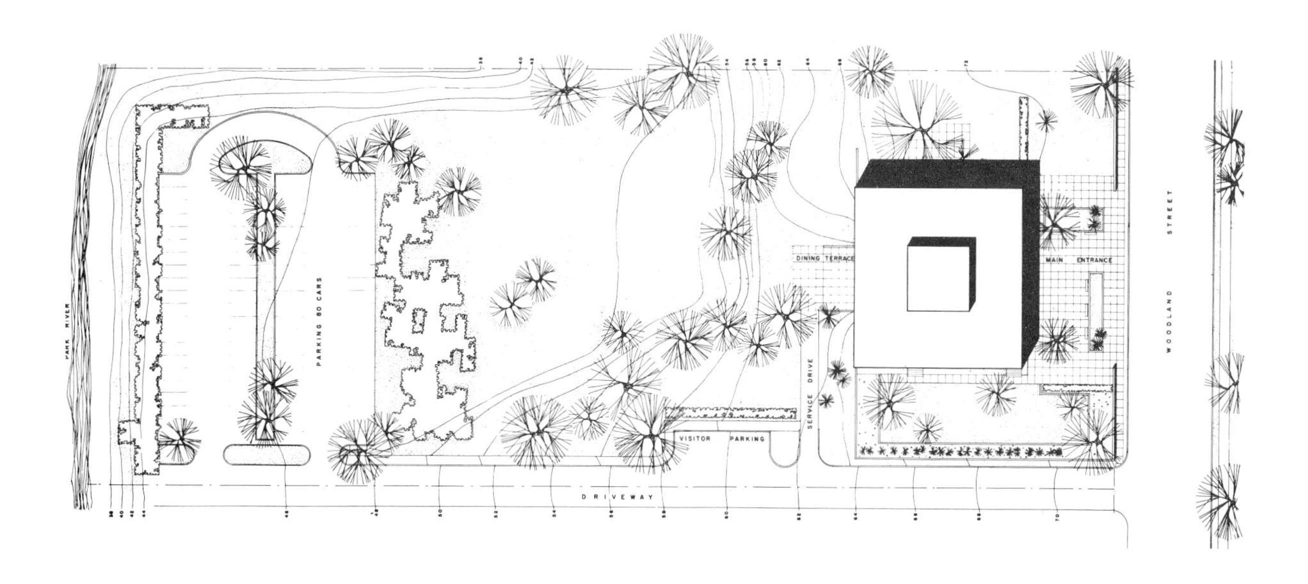
PARK RIVER
PARKING 80 CARS
DINING TERRACE
MAIN ENTRANCE
WOODLAND STREET
SERVICE DRIVE
VISITOR PARKING
DRIVEWAY

Minoru Yamasaki

Reynolds Metals Company

Great Lakes Sales Region Headquarters Building, Detroit, Michigan. 1961 Honor Award. Owner: Reynolds Metals Company. Photo: Baltazar Korab.

"Here," said the jury, "is a suburban answer, in poetic terms, which embraces both architecture and landscape design to the administrative requirements of American industry." Designed as a dramatic showcase for the architectural use of aluminum, this building has been hailed as "a sparkling example of Yamasaki's 'architecture of delight.'" The building is a three-story rectangle, containing sales offices and showroom, placed on a podium surrounded by a reflecting pool. The first floor is open, while the second and third floors are shielded on all four sides by a gold-anodized aluminium screen which gives it its jewel-like quality. Inside is an open well area, an atrium, covered with a skylight that consists of ninety-one glass-covered pyramids.

Skidmore, Owings & Merrill

Pepsi-Cola World Headquarters, New York City. 1961 Honor Award.

Owner: Pepsi-Cola Company. Photos: Ezra Stoller.

Not long ago the corporate image was architecturally reflected by stately columns and porticoes. Even skyscrapers borrowed ornamentation and knicknacks from archeology. Today that image is more often than not a sophisticated Miesian slab on stilts. This one combines the naked "functionalism" of the early moderns with elegant, classical proportion and a new emphasis on "liveability." Like Lever House (1952) by the same architects, this Park Avenue office building is raised on stilts to share part of its lobby space with the people on the street. It is also set back to make room for trees and other planting.

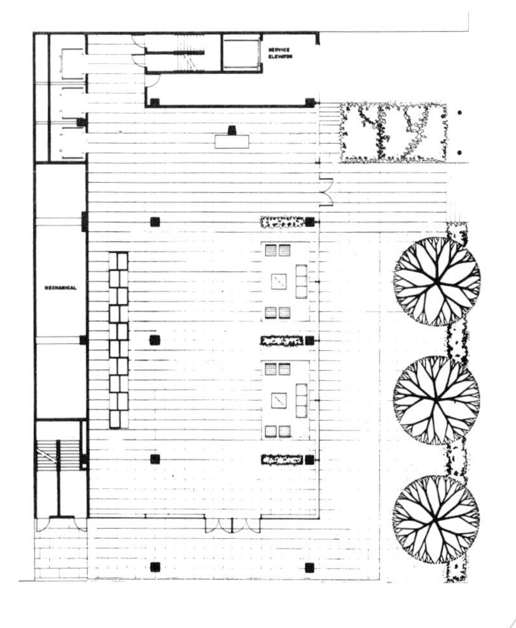
SERVICE ELEVATOR
MECHANICAL

2

COMMERCIAL BUILDINGS

Harold M. Heatley and Ketchum, Gina & Sharp

Davison-Paxon Company Store, Atlanta, Georgia. 1950 Honor Award.

Owner: Davison-Paxon Company, a subsidiary of R. H. Macy Company.

Photos: Hedrich-Blessing Studio.

To save the expense of underpinning the foundations of this building the architects, working with engineer Fred N. Severud, developed a bridge-like method of framing in which the tapered reinforced concrete columns, visible through the openings of the façade, are set back both from the front and the sides. The central area of each floor are thus unobstructed. The façade consists of a simple panel of reddish-brown brick surrounded by glass. Impulse, convenience, and demand merchandise is arranged inside in logical sequence, vertically and horizontally, in an atmosphere of simple elegance.

Davison's

Ketchum, Gina & Sharp

Wallachs Clothing Store, Jamaica, New York. 1949. Owner: Wallach, Inc. Photo: Lionel Freedman.

Welton D. Becket

Bullock's, Pasadena, California. 1947. Owner: Bullock's, Inc. Photo: Julius Shulman.

Welton D. Becket

Bercu Pipe Shop, Los Angeles, California. 1949. Photo: Julius Shulman.

Maynard Lyndon

Santa Fe City Ticket Office, Los Angeles, California. 1948. Owner: Atchison, Topeka & Santa Fe Railway. Photo: Merge Studios.

Prinz & Brooks

Oak Cliff Savings & Loan Association, Dallas, Texas. 1954. Photo: Ulric Meisel.

GENERAL TELEPHONE COMPANY
OF THE SOUTHWEST

Pace Associates

The General Telephone Company of the Southwest, San Angelo, Texas.
1955 Honor Award. Photos: Hedrich-Blessing.

At the request of the client the architects selected the site for this handsome building—ten acres in a new residential district with nearby schools and a shopping center—allowing for expansion, parking and landscaping. The low brick structure is a "good neighbor" to the adjacent homes and yet clearly and honestly states its special character and purpose. Pace Associates worked with Mies van der Rohe on the engineering, supervision, and budget determination of several important buildings, and his influence on this clean-cut structure is obvious.

McFarland, Bonsall & Thomas

Bank of Apple Valley, Apple Valley, California, 1953-54. Owner: Security-First National Bank. Photo: Douglas M. Simmonds.

Victor D. Gruen

Northland Regional Shopping Center, Southfield Township, Detroit, Michigan. 1954. Owner: Northland Center, Inc., subsidiary of J. L. Hudson Co. Photo: Ben Schnall.

William C. Muchow Associates

First Federal Savings and Loan Association, Denver, Colorado. 1954. Photo: Erwin Lang.

Stevens & Wilkinson

Rich's Department Store, Knoxville, Tennessee. 1955. Owner: Rich's Inc. Photo: Gottscho-Schleisner.

Weinberg & Teare

O'Neil Sheffield Shopping Center, Sheffield Township, Ohio. 1954. Owner: O'Neil Sheffield, Inc. Photo: R. Marvin Wilson.

Skidmore, Owings & Merrill

Manufacturer's Trust Company Fifth Avenue Branch, New York City. 1956 Honor Award. Owners: The Manufacturer's Trust Company. Photos: Ezra Stoller.

The glass sheets here are the largest used to date. Whereas most glass-walled buildings darkly reflect the outside, as in a mysterious, opaque mirror, this one truly fulfills the expectation of glass. It lets you look inside. The over-all luminous ceiling lighting, stronger than the natural light in the canyon of Fifth Avenue, does the trick. Never before has a bank been more open and inviting to its customers without sacrificing dignified solidity. Interior structural columns support the floor slabs, from which the exterior wall hangs in tension —a true curtain. The ground floor design focus is the gleeming safe-deposit vault. On the busy mezzanine, Harry Bertoia's large sculptural screen of golden steel adds sparkle and excitement. The building was limited to five stories because the adjacent building owns the "air rights" above 60 feet.

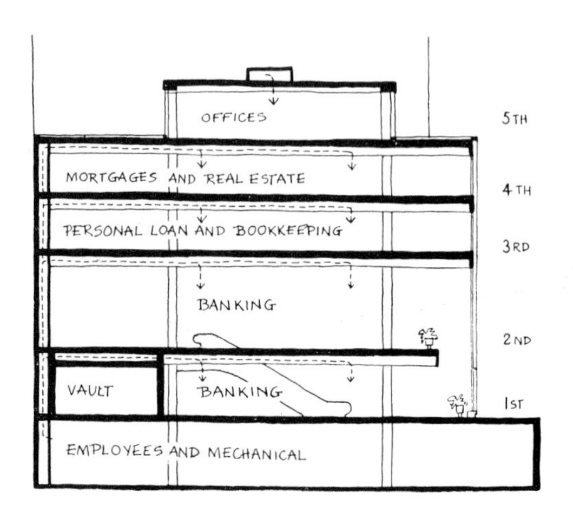

Hellmuth, Yamasaki & Leinweber

Lambert—St. Louis Municipal Airport Terminal Building, St. Louis, Missouri.

1956 Honor Award. Photos: Mac Mizuki and Hedrich-Blessing Studio.

Among the first of the dramatic new thin shell structures in the U. S., this terminal expresses the excitement of air travel. It consists of three pairs of intersecting concrete barrel vaults of 120-foot spans sprung from small point supports. Light pours into it through the glazed ends and sides as well as through the glass windows which carry over the top to where the adjoining concrete vaults touch each other. The low level of the hall contains freight and services. The middle level is for passengers.

IRLINES
INSURANCE INSURANCE
TRAL AIRLINES

Pereira & Luckman

Robinson's Specialty Shop, Palm Springs, California. 1958 Honor Award.

Photos: Julius Shulman.

Rising from a terraced and landscaped platform, this store achieves its pavilion-like appearance by means of a "floating" roof, supported independently of the non-load-bearing exterior walls. The building itself is composed of two distinct elements: the sales area, with a clear ceiling height of 14 feet; and a service area, including stockrooms, fitting rooms, offices, etc., with a 10-foot ceiling.

A specially designed tile of marble and quartz aggregate was used as veneer on exterior walls, with the diamond-shaped pattern repeated as a design motif throughout the building. Glass walls on the street frontages make the entire building a dramatic showcase for the merchandise within, and elevated light apertures above the main selling area provide even more daylight.

Weed, Johnson Associates

National Airlines Nose Hangar, Miami, Florida. 1958. Owner: Dade County Port Authority. Photo: Joseph B. Briguolo.

Mithun & Nesland

Washington State Bank, Bellevue Office, Bellevue, Washington. 1958. Photo: Charles R. Pearson.

Victor A. Lundy

Florida's Silver Springs (Tourist Center), Silver Springs, Florida. 1958. Owner: Ray, Davidson & Ray. Photo: Alexandre Georges.

Welton D. Becket and Associates; Rushmore & Woodman, Associate Architects

Tradewell Market, Burien, King County, Washington. 1959. Owner: Tradewell Stores, Inc. of Pacific Gamble Robinson Co., Seattle. Photo: Charles R. Pearson.

Toombs, Amisano & Wells

Lenox Square Shopping Center, Atlanta, Georgia. 1959. Owner: Samuel R. Noble Foundation. Photo: Gabriel Benzur.

3

HOTELS AND RESTAURANTS

Young, Richardson, Carleton and Detlie

Gaffney's Lake Wilderness, Maple Valley, Washington. 1952 Honor Award.

Owner: Gaffney's Lake Wilderness, Inc. Photos: Charles R. Pearson.

The architects of this resort lodge, on a magnificent lake in the shadow of Mount Rainier, adopted the principles of the modern house and connected the various rooms without partitioning them unnecessarily. The dining rooms, lounges, lobbies, cocktail lounge, mezzanine, and dining porches flow into each other, yet each maintains its identity. The *pièce de résistance* of the interior is a 35-foot totem pole, sculptured and gaily painted by Dudley Carter, an engineer turned artist. It serves as a roof column, supports the mezzanine, and adds to the memories of a truly magnificent vacation setting.

G. A. Downs

Apple Valley Inn, Apple Valley, California. 1953. Photo: Maynard L. Parker.

Skidmore, Owings & Merrill

Hilton Istanbul Hotel, Istanbul, Turkey. 1956. Photo: Ezra Stoller.

Victor A. Lundy

Warm Mineral Springs Inn, Venice, Florida. 1958. Photo: Alexandre Georges.

John Carl Warnecke

Mark Thomas Inn and Additions, Del Monte, Monterey, California. 1954-55. (Both received Awards of Merit.) Owner: Mr. Mark Thomas. Photo: Wynn Bullock.

Richard Dorman & Associates
Sidney M. Drasnin, Project Coordinator
Warren Waltz, Interiors

Ivory Tower Restaurant, Santa Monica, California. 1960. Owner: Leon Becker. Photo: Larry Frost.

4

PUBLIC BUILDINGS

William Henley Deitrick

North Carolina State Fair Pavilion, Raleigh, North Carolina. 1953 Honor Award. Owner: North Carolina Department of Agriculture. Photos: Joseph Molitor and L. R. Watson.

The design of this structure is parabolic in plan, section, and elevation. Two upward curving arches, 90 feet high, are supported on thin, vertical columns. The roof is hung on cables between the arches. Light floods the entire arena through heat- and glare-reducing glass walls. The arena holds 5,500 people on the seating stands and 4,000 on the floor. Below the seating stands are exhibition areas connected by passages around the sides. Dressing rooms, offices, and storage and mechanical facilities are on the basement level. Acoustic baffles, hung from the ceiling, have been added since this structure was photographed.

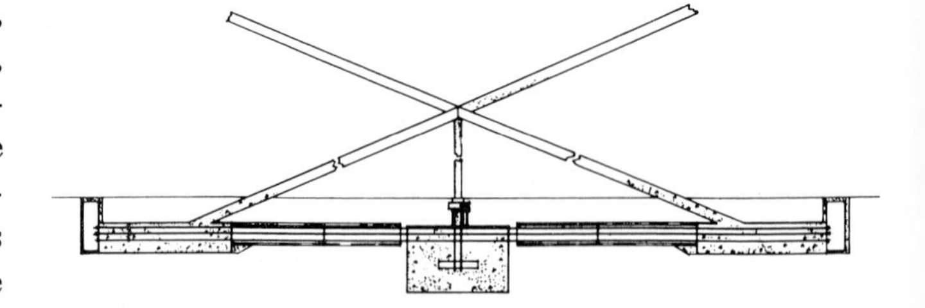

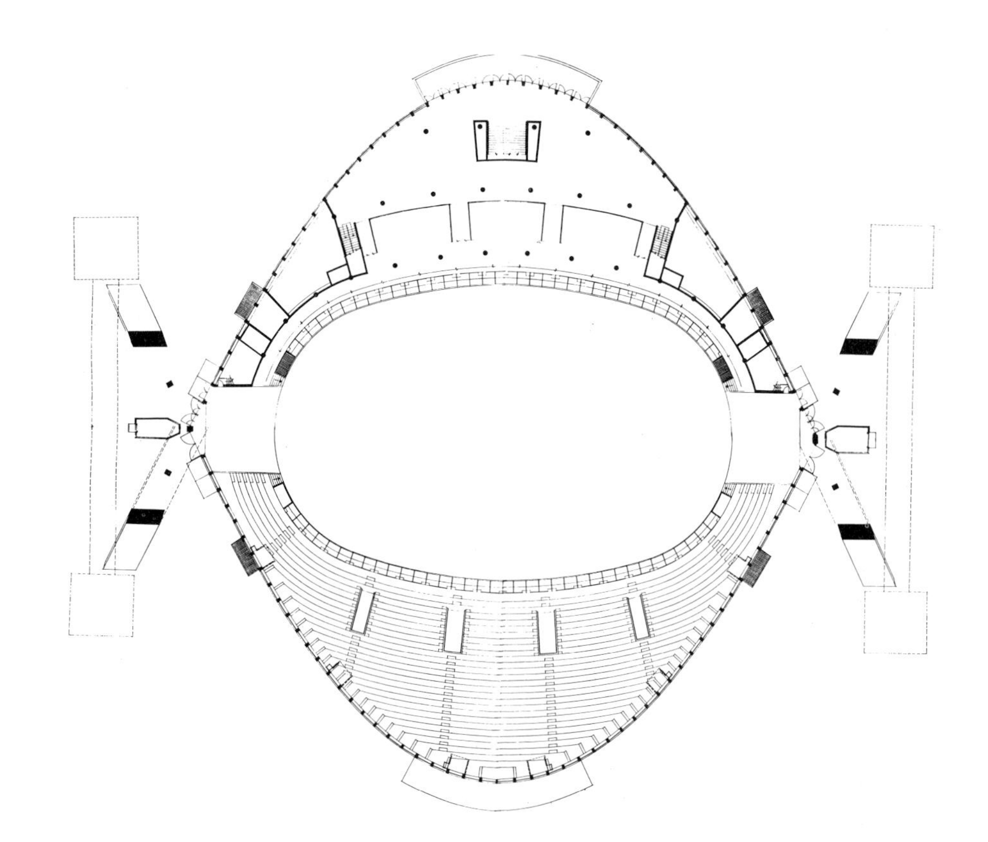

John P. Wiltshire and J. Herschel Fisher

Fort Brown Memorial Civic Center, Brownsville, Texas. 1954 Honor Award.

Owner: City of Brownsville, Texas. Photos: Ulric Meisel.

This center, a result of a state-wide architectural competition, is comprised of six public buildings: a youth center with game room, lounge, and snack bar; a 2,500-seat auditorium which can also be used as a gymnasium and multipurpose convention hall; a regulation size swimming pool; a library; a women's center, consisting of a lounge, a 75-seat meeting room, and kitchen; and a small 265-seat town hall. The appeal of this solution lies in its straightforward simplicity. As the jury remarked: "even a stranger could easily find his way around."

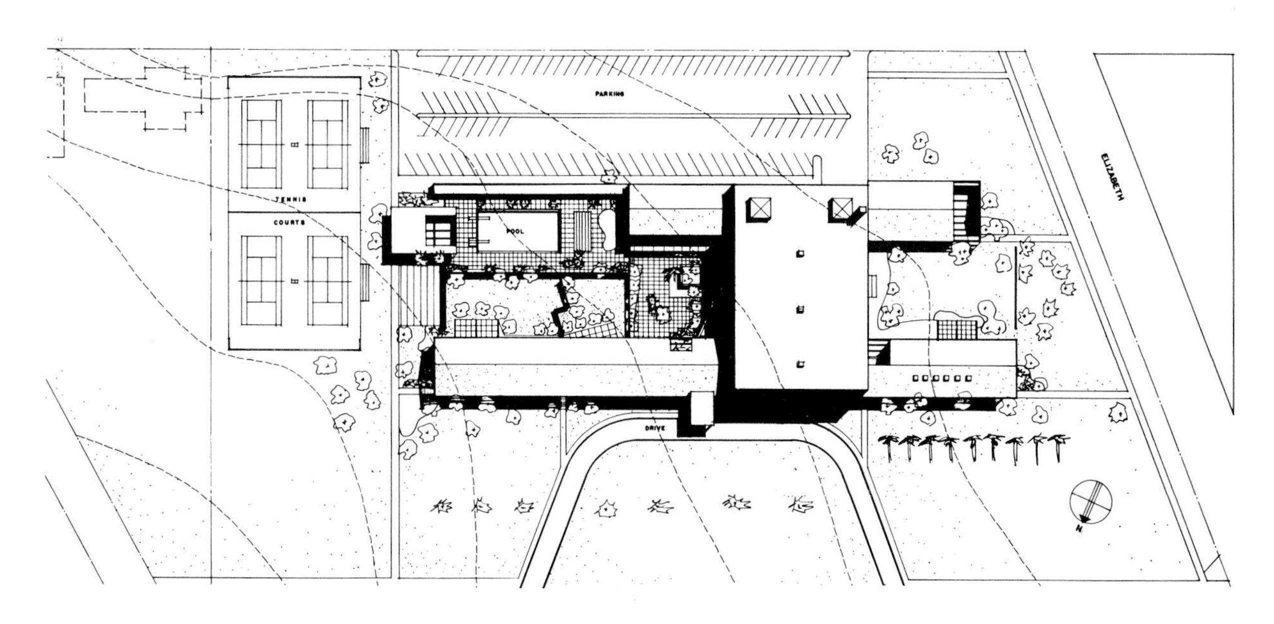
PARKING
TENNIS
COURTS
POOL
ELIZABETH
DRIVE
N

Freret & Wolf

Pontchartrain Beach Bus Shelter, New Orleans, Louisiana. 1948. Owner: Board of Levee Commissioners, Orleans Levee Board. Photo: Charles L. Franck.

Pereira & Luckman and J. E. Stanton
Robert W. Ditzen, Associate Architect

National Bureau of Standards, Boulder Laboratories, Boulder, Colorado. 1953. Owner: U. S. Government.

Rogers, Taliaferro & Lamb

Girl Scout Lodge, Camp Woodlands, Annapolis, Maryland. 1954. Owner: Girl Scouts of Anne Arundel County, Maryland. Photo: Marion E. Warren.

William B. Harvard

Bandstand and Park Pavilion, St. Petersburg, Florida. 1953. Photo: Abby.

Martin, Stewart & Noble

Mercantile Library, Philadelphia, Pennsylvania. 1954. Owner: The Free Library of Philadelphia. Photo: Cortlandt V. D. Hubbard.

Richard J. Neutra
Dion Neutra, Associate

Eagle Rock Playground Club House, Eagle Rock, California. 1954. Owner: City of Los Angeles. Photo: Julius Shulman.

Ralph Rapson and John Van Der Muhlen

United States Embassy, Stockholm, Sweden. 1955 Honor Award.

Owner: U. S. Department of State. Photos: Sune Sundahl.

Unpretentious yet attractive, this well-proportioned office building reflects the architects' belief that our embassies abroad must display to the world the image of a young and progressive nation. "It is impossible," says Rapson, "for our country to exercise political leadership without exercising a degree of cultural leadership as well. Our buildings abroad should be modern, friendly and inviting to properly express our attitude."

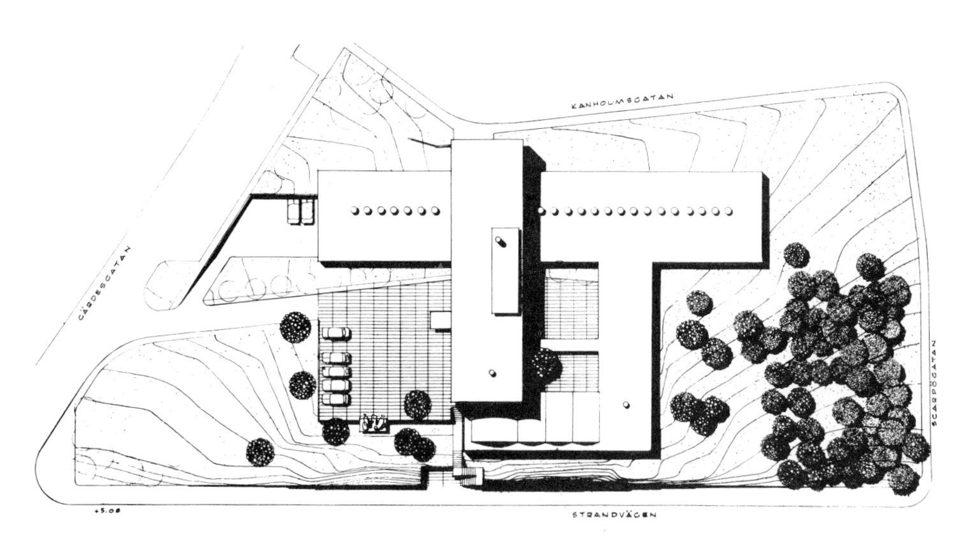
KANHOLMSGATAN
GÄRDESGATAN
SCARPÖGATAN
+5.08
STRANDVÄGEN

BRAZOS COUNTY

Caudill, Rowlett, Scott & Associates

Brazos County Courthouse and Jail, Bryan, Texas. 1957 Honor Award.

Photos: Roland Chatham.

This county building combines a friendly yet dignified appearance with unusual efficiency. It is planned almost like a campus: the county business and service offices—clerk, taxes, health, education, and welfare—are placed in expandable, individual units with separate entrances. The judicial functions—jail, courts, and offices—are arranged in a four-story unit. Lawbreakers and public are completely separated.

Welton Becket and Associates
J. E. Stanton, Associated Architect

Police Facilities Building, Civic Center,
Los Angeles, California. 1956. Owner:
City of Los Angeles. Photo: Julius Shulman.

Paul Thiry

Northeast Branch Public Library, Seattle,
Washington. 1954. Owner: Library Board,
City of Seattle. Photo: Art Hupy.

Antonin Raymond and L. L. Rado

Memorial Hall for Japanese Steel Workers, Kyushu, Japan. 1956. Owner: Workers Union, Yawata Steel Corporation.

Smith & Williams

Union Service Center, Los Angeles, California. 1957. Photo: Julius Shulman.

Eero Saarinen & Associates

United States Embassy Office Building, Oslo, Norway. 1960 Honor Award.

Owner: U. S. Department of State. Photos: K. Teigen.

The site is a triangular block with streets on three sides. The building faces the park-surrounded Royal Palace on Drammansviein Street, and the neighboring buildings, in Renaissance style, give the street a continuous façade and building line. Saarinen respected this and his checkerboard of wall frames, surfaced in greenish-black Norwegian granite, do not break the continuity. The skylighted, diamond-shaped interior court makes the elegance of the interior. This building is proof that an uncompromisingly modern structure can fit graciously and harmoniously into older surroundings. Nine out of ten Oslonians questioned by *Forum* magazine said they like the building and rank it with their own town hall, palace, and museums as one of their city's major attractions.

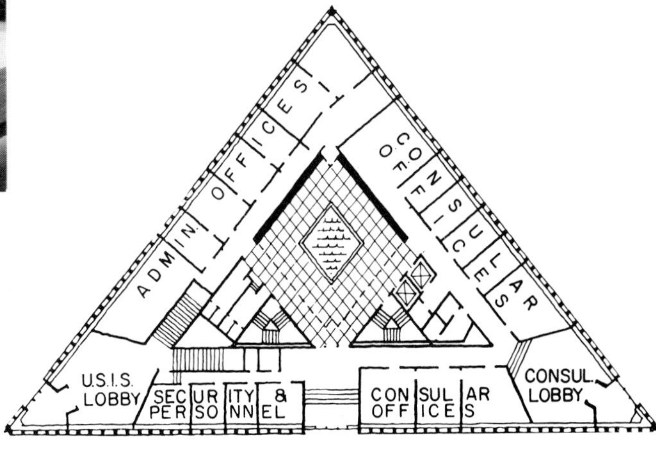

As attractive inside as it is outside, here is an excellent example of an architect's converting a liability (a small three-cornered lot) into a genuine asset. With offices occupying the perimeter, space was left in the center for service facilities and the handsome court.

Edward D. Stone

United States Pavilion, Universal and International Exposition, Brussels, Belgium. 1958.

Bay Group Associates (Daniel H. Bushnell; Lun Chan; Ichiro Sasaki; Camiel Van De Weghe)

Marin Bay Display Pavilion, San Rafael, California. 1960. Photo: Dandelet Photographs.

Corlett and Spackman   Kitchen and Hunt

Blyth Arena (Olympic Ice Arena), Squaw Valley, California. 1960 Honor Award.

Owner: United States (administered by Forest Service of the U. S. Dept. of Agriculture).

Photos: Phil Palmer (above) Rondal Partridge, and George Knight (at left).

The arena consists of two structures, one inside the other: The steel roof and the reinforced concrete grandstand. The steel girders which support the roof are connected to rigid backstays and masts. These hold cables on which the roof is suspended, allowing both a clear span of 300 feet and unbalanced loads of heavy snow. The roof deck is heated to reduce the snow, as is the adjacent trench which catches the snow sliding down. The south side of the arena is entirely open to afford a view of the speed skating rink and the ski jumps beyond. The bleacher seating units rotate to open further the arena for outside events. Here is an imaginative and gay structure whose flexibility of plan and airy quality well serves and reflects the activities for which it was designed. The same team of architects in association with a group of engineers also designed all other facilities for the 1960 Winter Olympics.

Edward D. Stone

United States Embassy, New Delhi, India. 1961 Honor Award. Owner: United States Department of State. Photos: Satayan.

Completed in January, 1959, our New Delhi Embassy is already "a modern classic." The decorative screen (which, of course, also serves a functional purpose in sunny India) envelopes a serenely composed building with a well-defined base, terminations, and cornice. There is, in contrast to so many contemporary buildings, no question where the entrance is. The covered inner court, with its pool and plantings, emphasizes modern architecture's new indoor-outdoor relationship. Most of all, however, this building is appropriate to the country in which it is a guest.

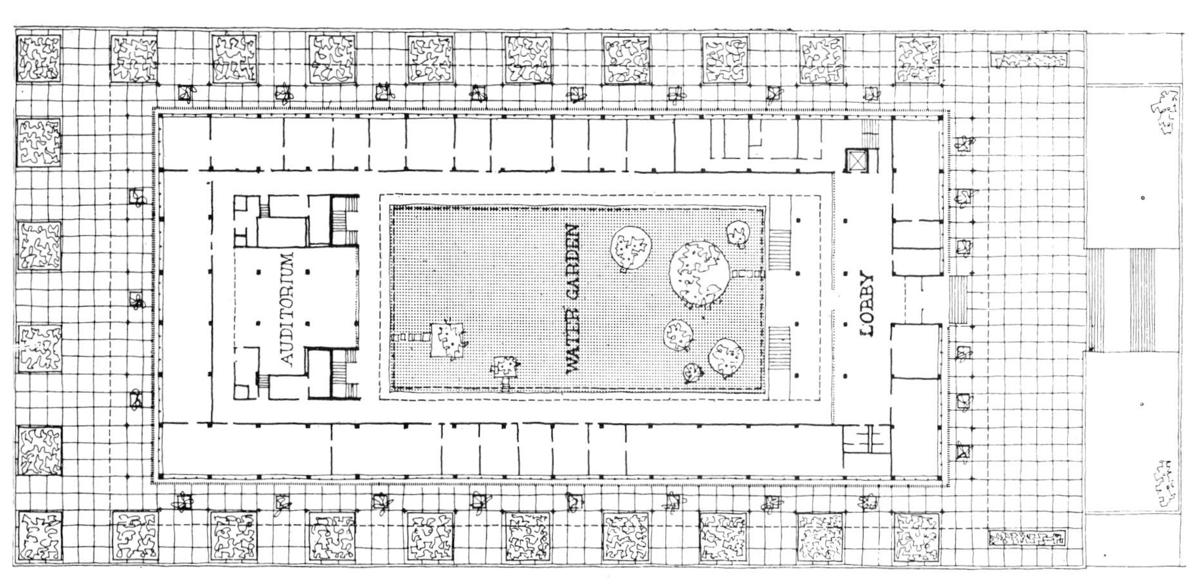

Main Floor Plan

5

INDUSTRIAL BUILDINGS

Stone & Pitts

Coca-Cola Bottling Plant, Houston, Texas. 1951 Honor Award. Owner: The Houston Coca-Cola Bottling Company. Photos: Harper Leiper Studios.

This is one of the world's largest bottling plants, handling 1,200 bottles per minute. In collaboration with the Coca-Cola Company's Engineering Department, the architects, departing from previous plant design, worked out new material-handling methods and machine layouts which achieved substantial savings in operating costs. With its rich variety of groupings, each frankly expressing its purpose, the building complex is well unified into a pleasing composition.

Francis Joseph McCarthy

Electronics Plant, San Carlos, California. 1951.

Owner: Frank G. Belcher.

Photo: Roger Sturtevant.

George Vernon Russell

Offices and Plant, Republic Supply Company, San Leandro, California. 1952.

Photo: Ernest Braun.

Harrison, Abramovitz & Abbe

Corning Glass Center, Corning, New York. 1951.
Owner: Corning Glass Works.
Photo: Ezra Stoller.

Skidmore, Owings & Merrill

Sawyer Biscuit Company Plant, Melrose Park, Illinois. 1953. Owner: United Biscuit Company of America. Photo: Hedrich-Blessing.

Eero Saarinen & Associates

Engineering Staff Buildings and Central Restaurant Building, General Motors Technical Center, Warren, Michigan. 1953 and 1955 Honor Awards. Photos: Ezra Stoller.

Two of the seventeen buildings on this world famous mile-square technological campus (begun in 1945 and completed in 1956) received AIA Honor Awards: the Engineering Staff Building, in 1953; and the Central Restaurant in 1955. Each of these buildings typifies one of the two central ideas which the Center as a whole expresses. The shops, drafting rooms, and offices of the former, flanking a pool, suggest strictly business. They are designed for clear thinking and are themselves an industrial product. The latter, in contrast, subjects technical precision to human amenity. It has been designed for people who walk, relax, and

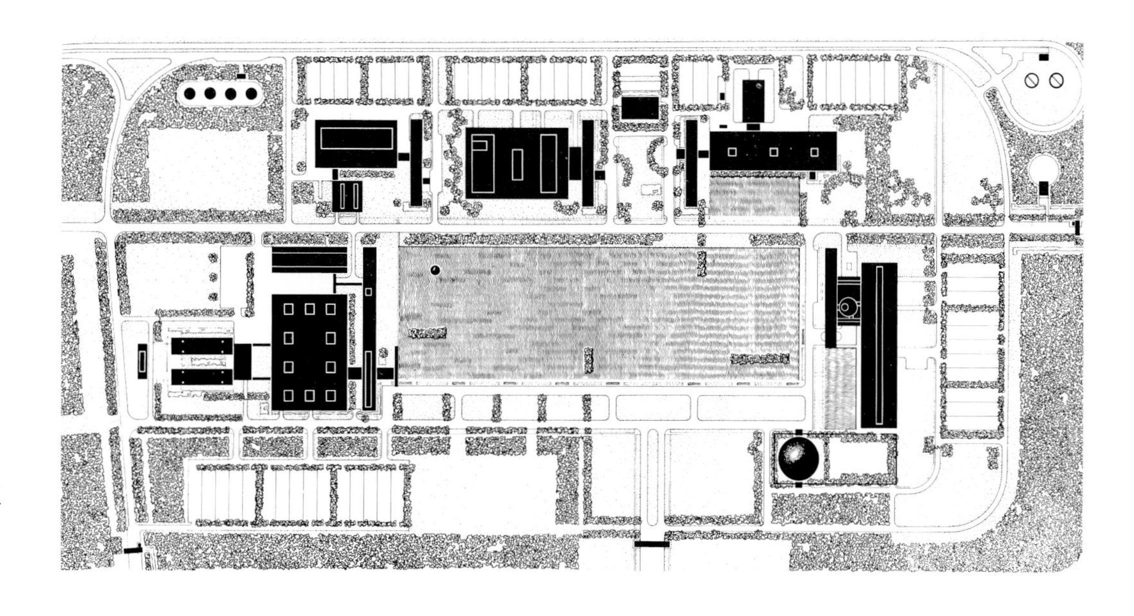

need a change of pace from their work. The dining area is raised to afford a view across a tree-studded court to the lake and the distant fountain. It is further separated from the entrance by sculptor Harry Bertoia's golden glinting screen, a forerunner of the one he created for the Manufacturer's Trust Company in New York. The most outstanding feature of the Center, which these pictures cannot convey, is not the efficiency and sophistication of its building materials and mechanical devices but the rich, romantic use of color, particularly in the royal blue and crimson glazed brick end walls.

Edward D. Stone

The Stuart Company, Pasadena, California. 1958 Honor Award.

Owner: Arthur O. Hanisch. Photos: Julius Shulman.

President Arthur Hanisch of the Stuart Company, a pharmaceutical manufacturer, wanted a combination plant and office building which would instill in his 160 employees a sense of participation. He achieved it, by giving his architect entirely free rein—even to the point of refusing to go and look at the building until it was finished. Set back 150 feet from a busy highway, the building's front façade is one story. Then the grade drops to form a two-story building. Offices, laboratories, and manufacturing rooms are grouped around a garden court and dining lounge which opens to an outdoor swimming pool and recreation area on the lower level. In addition to being luxuriously attractive and coolly efficient, the building disproves the common idea that a handsome commercial building necessarily costs more than an ugly one. The company reportedly saved about $13 per square foot as against what a conventionally designed structure might have cost.

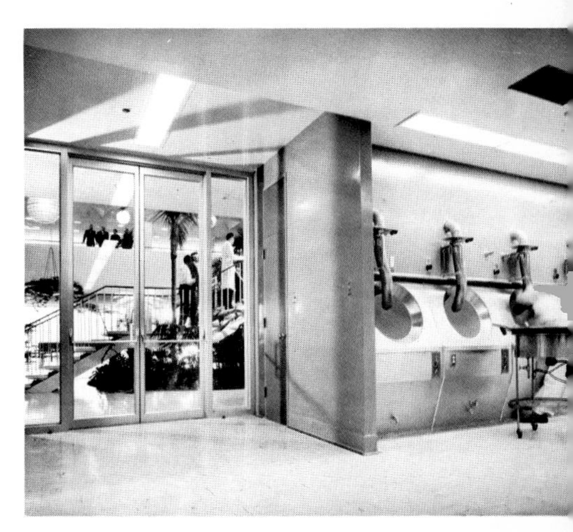

Isidor Richmond and Carney Goldberg

Refuse Incinerator, Town of Brookline, Massachusetts. 1954.
Photo: Joseph W. Molitor.

Skidmore, Owings & Merrill

Wyeth Laboratories, Inc., Radnor, Pennsylvania. 1957. Photo: Ezra Stoller.

Pereira & Luckman

Beckman/Helipot Corporation Plant, Newport Beach, California. 1956.
Photo: Julius Shulman.

Skidmore, Owings & Merrill

Industrial Reactor Laboratories, Plainsborough, New Jersey. 1958. Photo: Alexandre Georges.

Weed-Johnson-Associates

Office & Warehouse for The Coppertone Corporation, Miami, Florida. 1950. Photo: Baker-Black.

Philip Johnson

Nuclear Reactor, Rehovot, Israel. 1961 Honor Award.

Owner: Government of Israel.

For a time it appeared that Philip Johnson was the chief prophet of Miesian purity. His own "glass cage" house at New Canaan, Connecticut (1949), even surpassed the master in utter simplicity: a single space defined only by the brick floor, the roof, the steel columns, and the glazed wall, divided almost exclusively by the furniture. In the late fifties, however, Johnson suddenly moved on to bend this style to more expressive, sculptural forms. Reminiscent of Eric Mendelsohn's visionary sketches of 1919, this still simple structure is not intimidated by the complex, technological appurtenances it houses. It masters them with calm, human design. A monument rather than a mechanical contrivance, this building makes bold of the play of light and shadow and the rich texture of its concrete.

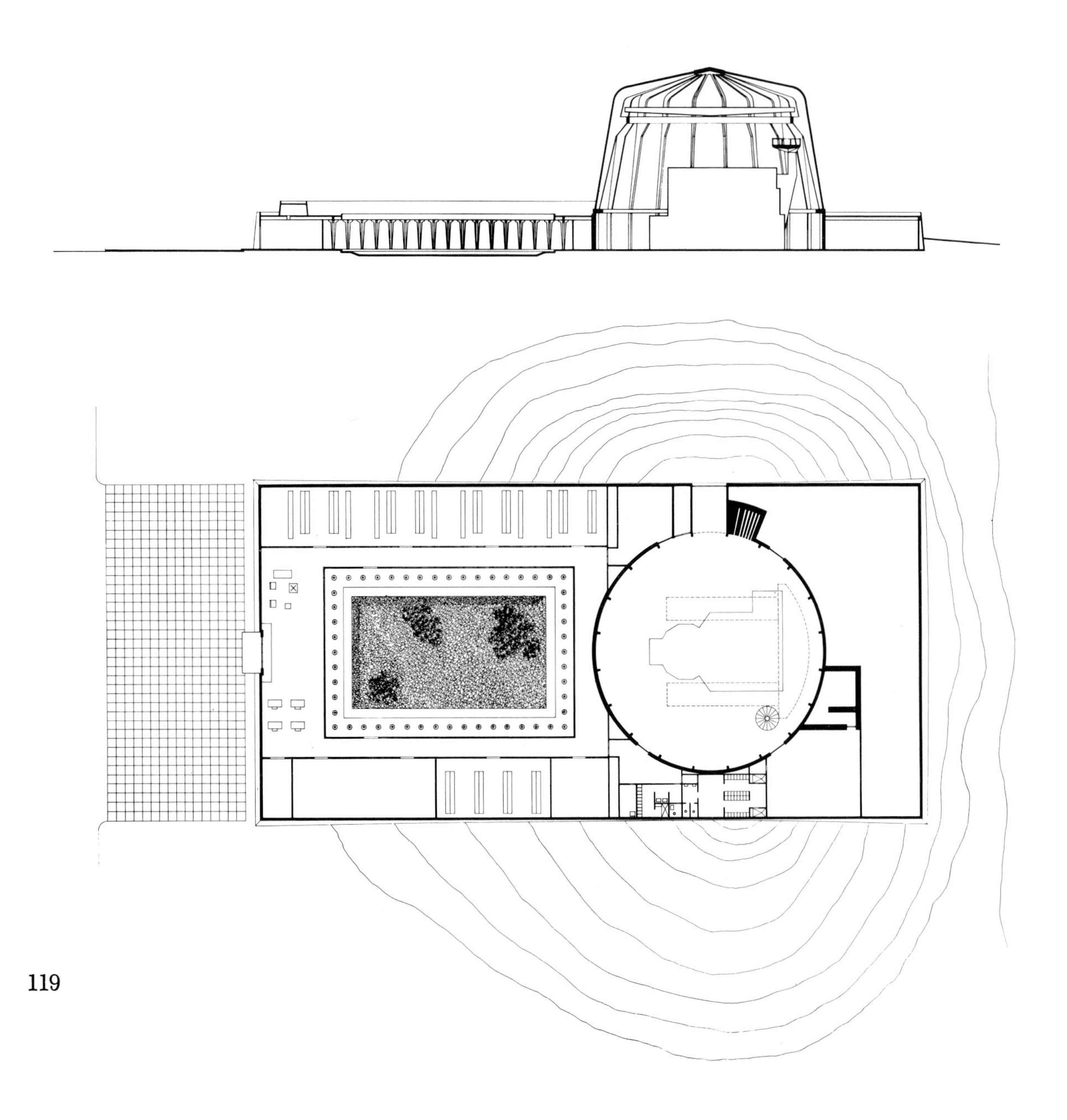

6

MEDICAL BUILDINGS

Thorshov & Cerny

Clearwater County Memorial Hospital, Bagley, Minnesota. 1951 Honor Award.

Owner: Clearwater County Memorial Hospital. Photos: Warren Reynolds, Infinity, Inc.

The starting point for the architects of this small, self-contained general hospital was the view through a grove of pine trees over the lake. All thirty patients, except for those in the isolation suite, can enjoy it. All the facilities are on one floor in a compact and efficient arrangement. The nurses' station is in a central "command" position, yet immediately adjacent to the public and ambulance entrance and lobby. This is particularly convenient at night when the staff is reduced.

LAUNDRY
OPERATING
DELIVERY
MECH EQUIP
LINEN
SCRUB
CLEAN UP
JAN
STORE
CENTRAL STERILE SUPPLY
LABOR
ANESTHESIA STORAGE
AMBULANCE ENTRANCE
VEST
STRETCHER
DOCTORS LOCKERS
SUPTS OFFICE
SERVICE ENTRANCE
EMERGENCY TREATMENT
OFFICE
X-RAY
COLD ST
KITCHEN
DARK ROOM
CONT
DRESS
LABORATORY
VISITORS ENTRANCE
LOBBY
ISOLATION
DISHWASHING
NURSES LOCKERS
NURSERY
WORK
ISOL'N NURSERY
BATH
DINING
UTILITY
NURSES STATION
MED
BED PAN
TEL
ANTE RM
SUB-UTIL
DAY ROOM

Schmidt, Garden & Erikson

Xavier Hospital, Dubuque, Iowa. 1949. Owners: Sisters of St. Francis of the Holy Family. Photo: Link.

Sherlock, Smith & Adams

Perry County Hospital, Marion, Alabama. 1951. Owner: Perry County Hospital Board. Photo: Betty Baldwin.

Stevens & Wilkinson

Georgia Baptist Hospital, Atlanta, Georgia. 1951. Photo: Jerome Drown.

Pohlmeyer & Pohlmeyer
Skidmore, Owings & Merrill, Associate Architects

Northern Indiana Hospital for Children, South Bend, Indiana. 1951. Photo: Torkel Korling.

Giffels & Vallet, Inc.
A. M. Strauss,
Associated Architect

U. S. Veterans Administration Hospital, Fort Wayne, Indiana. 1950. Owner: U. S. Government. Photo: Lens-Art Photographers.

Allison and Rible

Goodyear Memorial Pavilion, Ventura, California. 1951. Owner: Foster Memorial Hospital. Photo: William Aplin.

Steele, Sandham & Steele
Alex Weinstein, Associate

St. Vincent's Home for the Aged,
Omaha, Nebraska. 1953.
Owner: Sisters of Mercy.
Photo: Walter L. Griffith, Jr.

Golemon & Rolfe

St. Frances Cabrini Hospital, Alexandria, Louisiana. 1951. Owner: Sisters of Charity of the Incarnate Word, Houston, Texas. Photo: Paul Dorsey.

Skidmore, Owings & Merrill

Illinois Children's Home & Aid Society,
Chicago, Illinois. 1949.
Photo: Torkel Korling, Hedrich-Blessing.

Kelly & Gruzen and Isadore Rosenfield

U. S. Veterans Administration Hospital, Wilkes-Barre, Pennsylvania. 1950. Owner: U. S. Government. Photo: Ben Schnall.

Stone and Mulloy; Marraccini and Patterson

Peninsula Memorial Blood Bank, Burlingame, San Mateo County, California. 1954. Owner: Board of Directors, Peninsula Memorial Blood Bank.
Photo: Karl H. Riek.

Milton Foy Martin

Texas Children's Hospital, Texas Medical Center, Houston, Texas. 1954. Photo: Harper Leiper Studios.

Vincent G. Kling

The Lankenau Hospital, Philadelphia, Pennsylvania.

1954 Honor Award. Photo: Lawrence S. Williams.

Deliberately reminiscent of a sedate resort hotel, this trend-setting hospital commands the highest ground of a former golf course in suburban Philadelphia. It is composed of three principal elements: a six-story, 350-bed nursing wing facing towards the view; a smaller parallel wing for out-patient clinics and doctors' offices; and a connecting "stem" with operating and delivery rooms, diagnostic and therapy rooms, laboratories, and administrative offices. The building program placed major emphasis on facilities for *preventing* illness. Kling's solution, with its cheerful elegance and careful attention to the natural environment, is designed to speed recovery.

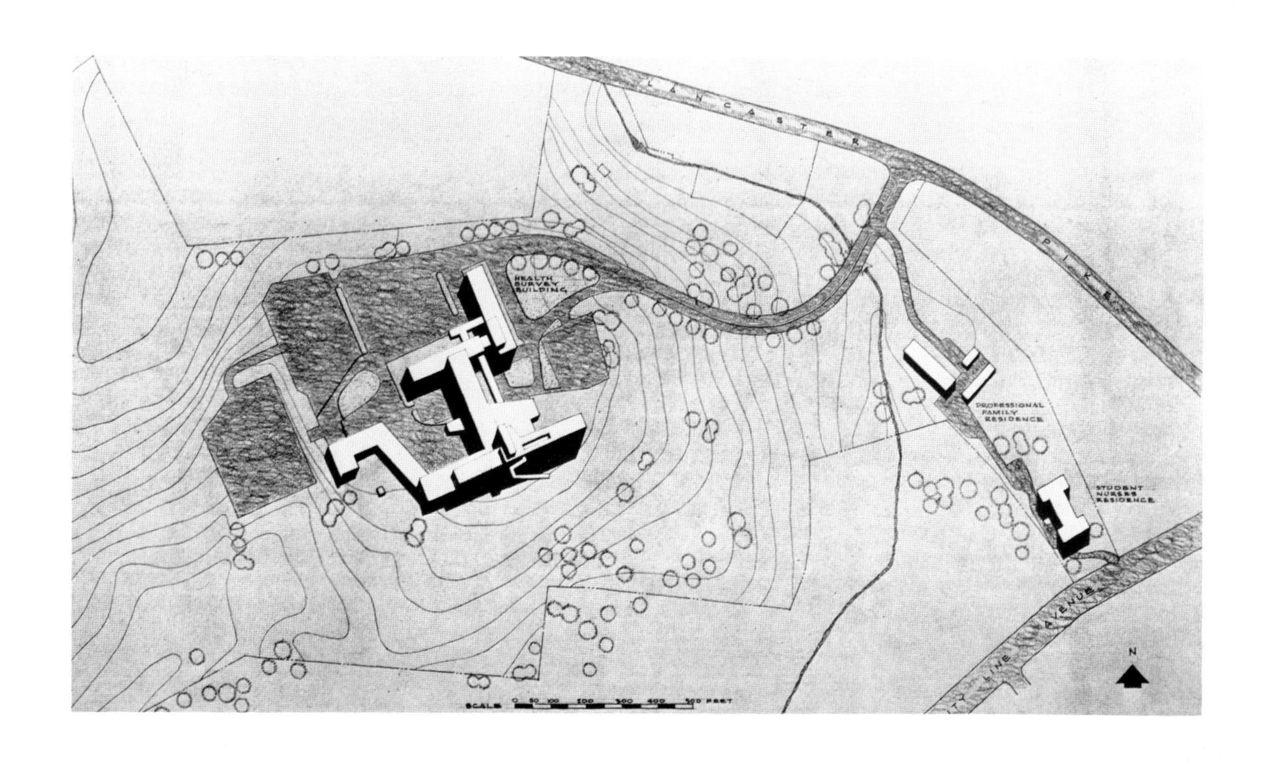
LANCASTER
PIKE
HEALTH
SURVEY
BUILDING
PROFESSIONAL
FAMILY
RESIDENCE
STUDENT
NURSES
RESIDENCE
AVENUE
N
SCALE 0 50 100 200 300 400 500 FEET

Charles R. Colbert of Colbert and Lowrey and Associates

Diaz-Simon Pediatric Clinic, New Orleans, Louisiana. 1959 Honor Award.

Owners: Drs. Joseph A. Diaz and Henry G. Simon. Photo: Frank Lotz Miller.

A clinic for four pediatricians and a maximum of off-street parking space for their patients' parents (required by ordinance) had to be accommodated on a small (35′ x 125′) lot on a modest budget. Ingenious organization solved the problem with considerable architectural distinction. The cars are parked below the elevated building. The waiting room includes the staircase, and offices and examination rooms are easily accessible. The required front-yard setback was used for an attractive sculptural court.

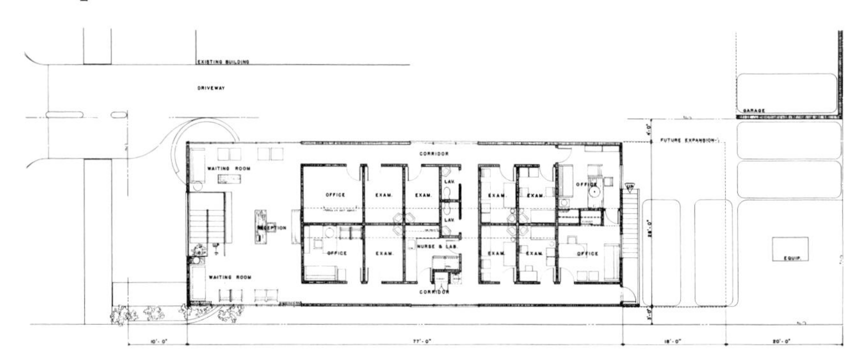

DIAZ - SIMON
PEDIATRIC CLINIC

Curtis & Davis

Our Lady of the Sea General Hospital, Golden Meadow, Louisiana. 1955. Owner: Lafourche Parish Hospital Service, District No. 1. Photo: Frank Lotz Miller.

Yamasaki, Leinweber and Associates

David Feld Medical Clinic, Detroit, Michigan. 1954. Owners: Harry Weisberg, David Feld, and Jack Weisberg. Photo: Lens-Art Photographers.

Curtis & Davis

Sako Clinic for Children (Children's Clinic), Raceland, Louisiana. 1954. Owner: Dr. Wallace Sako. Photo: Frank Lotz Miller.

7

RELIGIOUS BUILDINGS

Smith and Williams

Children's Chapel, Neighborhood Church, Pasadena, California. 1954. Photo: Julius Shulman.

James M. Hunter

Danforth Chapel, Colorado A. and M. College, Fort Collins, Colorado. 1954. Photo: Warren Reynolds of Infinity, Inc.

Chaix & Johnson

St. Brigid Catholic Church, Los Angeles, California. 1954. Owner: Roman Catholic Archdiocese of Los Angeles.
Photo: Alexander Hovsepian.

A. Quincy Jones & Frederick E. Emmons

St. Matthews Episcopal Church, Pacific Palisades, California. 1953.
Photo: Julius Shulman.

Anshen and Allen

Chapel of the Holy Cross, Sedona, Arizona. 1957 Honor Award. Donated to the Roman Catholic Church by Marguerite Staude in memory of her father and mother, Mr. and Mrs. Lucien Brunswig. Photos: Julius Shulman.

Wedged into a spur of deep red sandstone, one hundred feet above the plain of the Verde River Valley, a symbol has here become architecture. Its simple linear design contrasts sharply with nature's jagged sculpture. The chapel's foot-thick concrete shell is sandblasted and colored to a rich, textured finish. The two ends are of smoke-colored glass to diminish glare and permit the congregation of fifty a clear view of the magnificent panorama beyond the altar. The interior face of the 90-foot cross carries the Corpus wrought in iron by Keith Monroe, a San Francisco sculptor.

Antonin Raymond and L. L. Rado

St. Anselm's Priory for the Benedictine Fathers, Tokyo, Japan. 1957 Honor Award.

The side walls and roof of this church are of reinforced concrete, folded in accordion fashion for added strength, and poured in metal forms for a marble smooth surface. Parts of the exposed concrete have been dye-stained with transparent washes of earthy colors—Indian red, Siena ochre, gray-green, charcoal gray, and light blue for parts of the ceiling. The rich color of the floors and stained glass windows and of the furnishings, and artifacts, designed by the architect and his wife, further enhance this synthesis of form and color, creating an effect of serenity and grandeur. But artifacts and decorations aside, this space alone has a devout atmosphere—a something that was not put there. The church is flanked on one side by the L-shaped school and assembly hall facing a play court and on the other by a future cloister—all linked by covered walks.

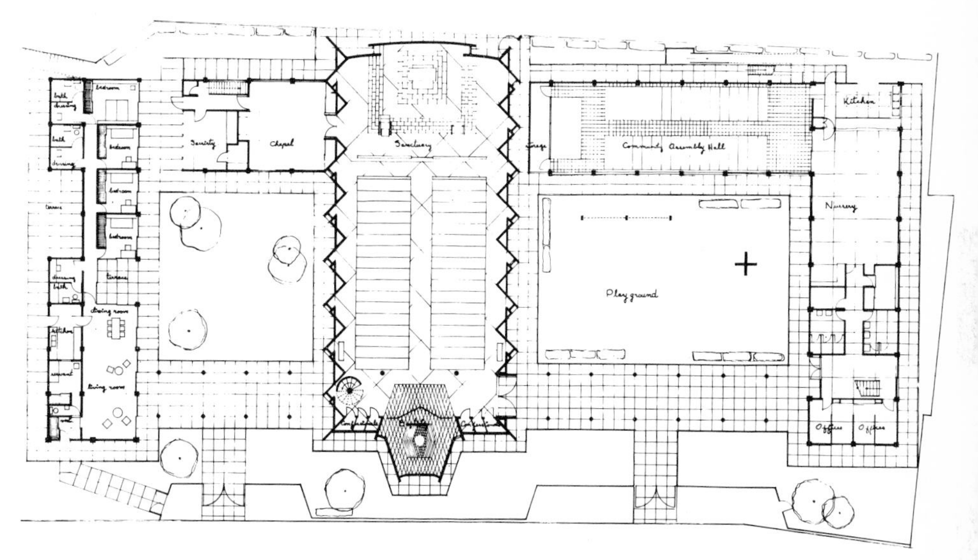

Alden B. Dow

First Methodist Church,
Midland, Michigan. 1949.
Photo: Hedrich-Blessing.

Lawrence & Saunders

Gretna Methodist Church,
Gretna, Louisiana. 1959.
Photo: Frank Lotz Miller.

Harrison & Abramovitz

Interfaith Center, Brandeis
University, Waltham,
Massachusetts. 1955.
Photo: Ezra Stoller.

Curtis and Davis
Harrison Schouest, Associated Architect

Immaculate Conception Church, Marrero, Louisiana. 1957. Photo: Frank Lotz Miller.

Howard R. Meyer and Max M. Sandfield, Associated Architects
William W. Wurster, Consulting Architect

Temple Emanu-El, Dallas, Texas. 1957. Photo: Ulric Meisel.

Philip Johnson

Roofless Church, New Harmony, Indiana. 1961 Honor Award. Owner: Robert Lee Blaffer Trust. Photos: George Holton.

The dome has here taken on a new form. It defines space rather than encloses it. It may well be that this lyrical statement by Philip Johnson contradicts the contention that our time is too poor in poetic emotion to produce monuments. This one, on the banks of the Wabash, is dedicated to the Rappites, who believe in the imminent second coming of Christ and who founded Harmony as a utopian religious community early in the nineteenth century. Set in a 130 x 230 foot walled temple garden, the "Roofless Church" consists of a 50-foot-high gently undulating parabolic dome of laminated pine arches resting lightly on limestone piers. It is covered with rough cedar shakes and shelters "The Virgin," a bronze by Jacques Lipchitz.

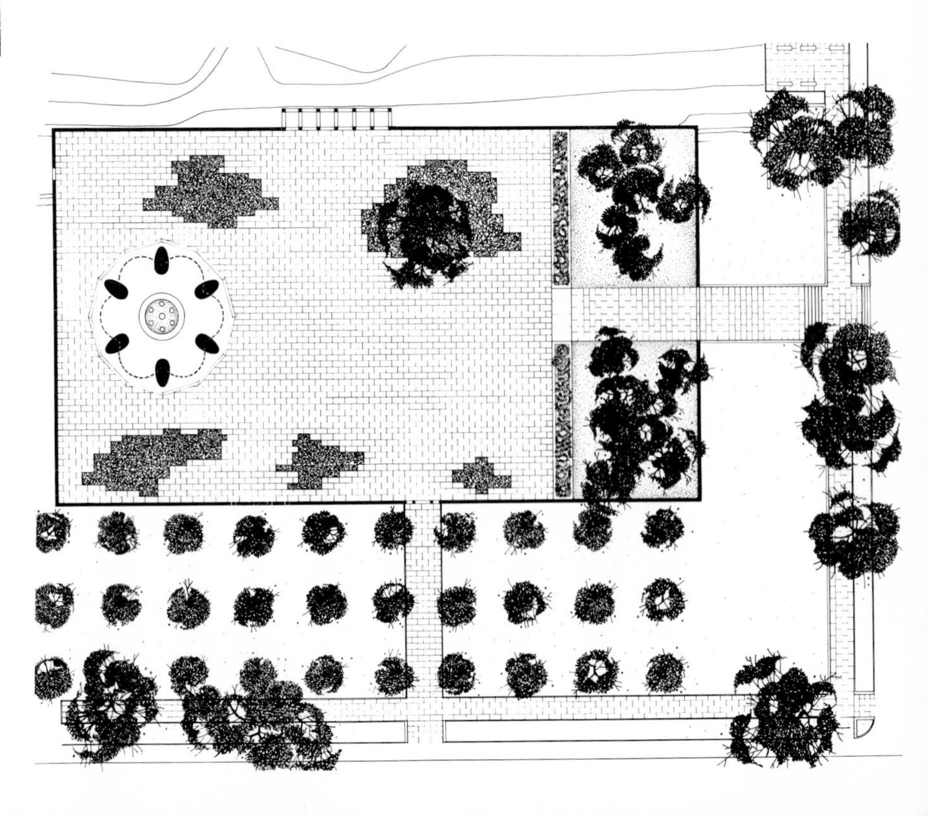

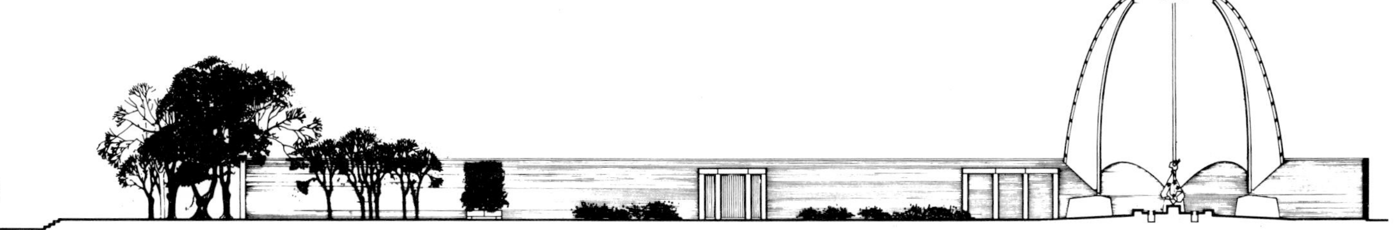

Pietro Belluschi and Rogers, Taliaferro & Lamb, Associated Architects

The Church of the Redeemer, Baltimore, Maryland. 1958. Photo: Joseph W. Molitor.

Victor A. Lundy

St. Paul's Lutheran Church (Fellowship Hall), Sarasota, Florida. 1960. Photo: George Cserna.

Milton A. Ryan

First Church of Christ, Scientist, Victoria, Texas. 1952. Photo: Ulric Meisel.

Hugh Stubbins and Associates

The Unitarian Church, Concord, New Hampshire. 1960. Owner: The Second Congregational Society (Unitarian) of Concord. Photo: Maris-Ezra Stoller Assocs.

Henry Hill; John W. Kruse, Associate

Chapel, Moline Public Hospital, Moline, Illinois. 1960. Photo: Roger Sturtevant.

Wallace Neff

Manresa Jesuit Retreat House , Azusa, California. 1955. Photo: Shirley Burdon.

8

CAMPUS BUILDINGS

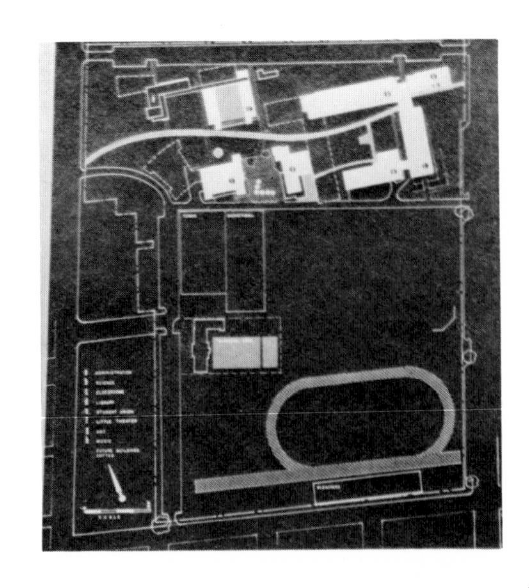

Smith, Powell & Morgridge

Santa Monica City College, Santa Monica, California. 1954 Honor Award.

Photos: Fred R. Dapprich.

This college serves a geographically limited district. It did not, therefore, have to be planned for almost unlimited expansion. The buildings could be arranged in a compact series of quadrangles and courts, which form the heart of the group. The students can move freely from building to building in a garden-like setting. The group includes a theater and a large gymnasium adjacent to the city-owned plunge.

Neutra and Alexander

Business Education Building, Orange Coast College, Costa Mesa, California. 1953.
Owner: Board of Trustees of the Orange Coast College District.
Photo: Julius Shulman.

Lundgren & Maurer

Pi Kappa Alpha Fraternity House, Austin, Texas. 1951.
Owner: Beta Mu Chapter of Pi Kappa Alpha Fraternity.
Photo: Dewey Mears.

Michael Goodman

Biochemistry and Virus Laboratory, Berkeley, California. 1952.
Owner: Regents of the University of California.
Photo: Mason Weymouth.

Clark and Beuttler

Home Economics Building, University of California, Davis, California. 1952. Owner: Regents of the University of California. Photo: Ernest Braun.

Skidmore, Owings & Merrill

Service Schools, Great Lakes, Illinois (Naval Training Center Service Schools; Gunners' Mates Building; Fire Control Technicians Building). 1954. Owner: U. S. Navy. Photo: Hedrich-Blessing.

Jan Hird Pokorny

The William H. and May D. Taylor Memorial Library and the John M. Reeves Student Building, Hackettstown, New Jersey. 1954. Owner: Centenary College for Women. Photo: Ben Schnall.

Eero Saarinen & Associates

Women's Dormitories and Dining Hall, Drake University, Des Moines, Iowa.

1955 Honor Award. Photos: Reynolds Photography, Inc.

The master plan for this campus was developed by the late Eliel Saarinen. His son, Eero, with Joseph N. Lacy, evolved the buildings. To preserve the natural charm of the site, the architect introduced small foot bridges to span the ravine and facilitate circulation. The dormitories are of tilt-up slab construction—concrete wall panels, poured on the ground and hoisted in place as both exterior walls and interior partitions. The exterior is faced with brick. The social rooms are separately framed two-story structures attached to each dormitory. The dining hall is similarly constructed at the highest point of the site. Serving the entire campus, the main dining room is located on the second floor to take advantage of the view.

parking
bridge
DORMITORY No 1
social room
DORMITORY No 2
social room
bridge
pool
bridge
bridge
DORMITORY No 3
social room
DINING HALL
parking
service drive

Wurster, Bernardi & Emmons

Center for Advanced Study in Behavioral Sciences, Palo Alto, California.

1956 Honor Award. Owner: Center for Advanced Study in Behavioral Sciences, Inc.

Photos: Morley Baer.

To this "scientific monastery," as it has been called, the Center invites scholars in a number of sciences dealing with the behavior of man to spend a paid sabbatical studying and exchanging views and ideas. The architects have provided a most sympathetic environment for both these pursuits: ideal study rooms and congenial public rooms for seminars, meetings, conversation, and dining. The study buildings are placed around the cross-shaped central building, creating two major courts and several minor ones, all most attractively landscaped by landscape architect Thomas D. Church.

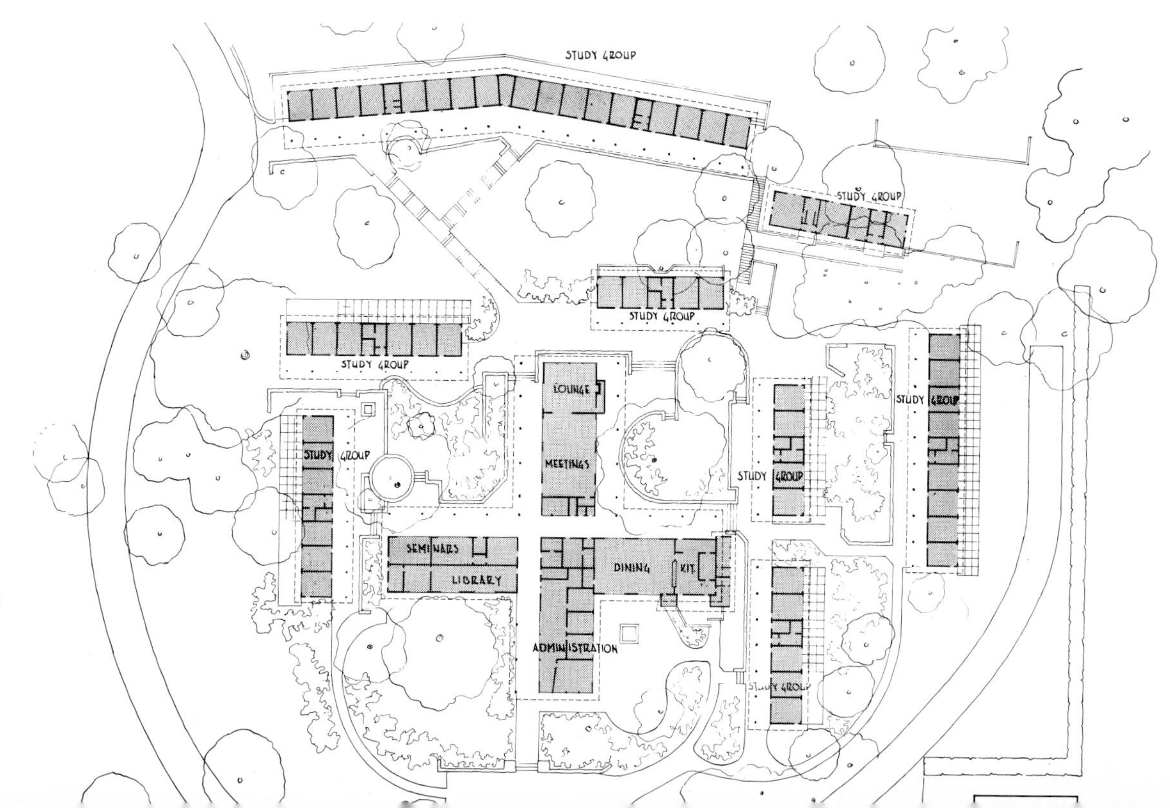

STUDY GROUP
STUDY GROUP
STUDY GROUP
STUDY GROUP
LOUNGE
STUDY GROUP
STUDY GROUP
MEETINGS
STUDY GROUP
SEMINARS
LIBRARY
DINING
KIT
ADMINISTRATION
STUDY GROUP

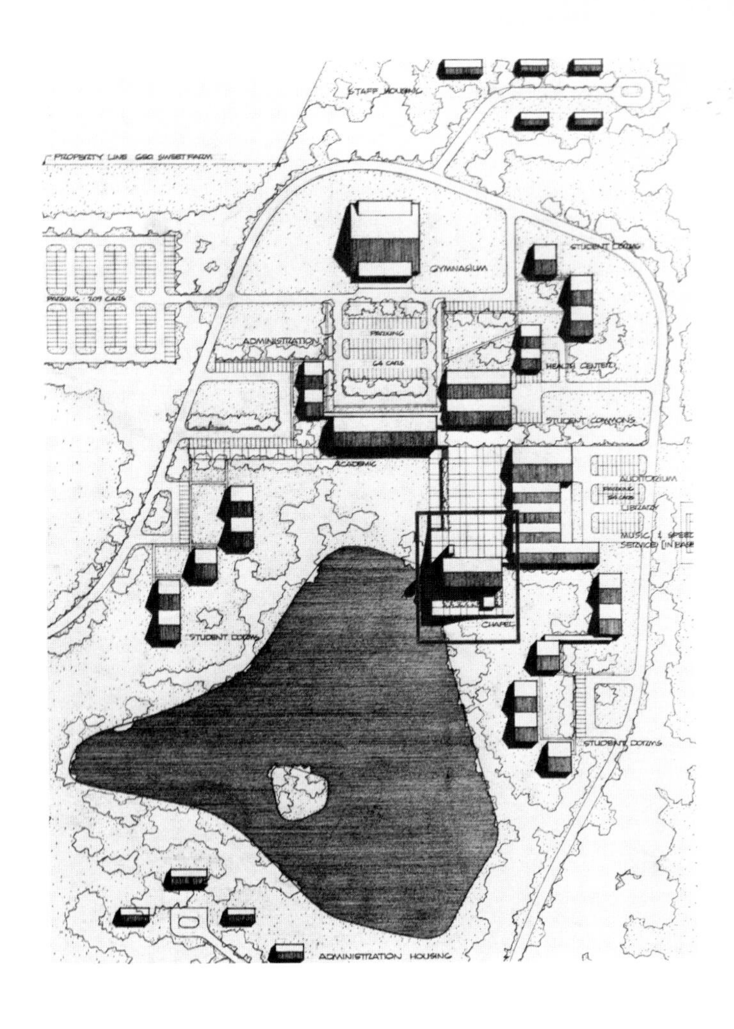
STAFF HOUSING
PROPERTY LINE
GYMNASIUM
STUDENT DORMS
PARKING 209 CARS
ADMINISTRATION
PARKING
64 CARS
HEALTH CENTER
STUDENT COMMONS
ACADEMIC
AUDITORIUM
LIBRARY
CHAPEL
STUDENT DORMS
STUDENT DORMS
ADMINISTRATION HOUSING

Eero Saarinen & Associates

Concordia Senior College, Fort Wayne, Indiana. 1959 Honor Award.

Owner: Lutheran Church, Missouri Synod. Photo: Alexandre Georges.

The site plan for this small college for divinity students recalls a North European village. The chapel, placed on the highest spot, dominates the casual yet serene grouping of the other buildings. Its black pitched roof is echoed by them, giving the entire campus a rare unity of expression. Without straining for originality and with very simple means, Saarinen has here achieved an architecture of great dignity and power.

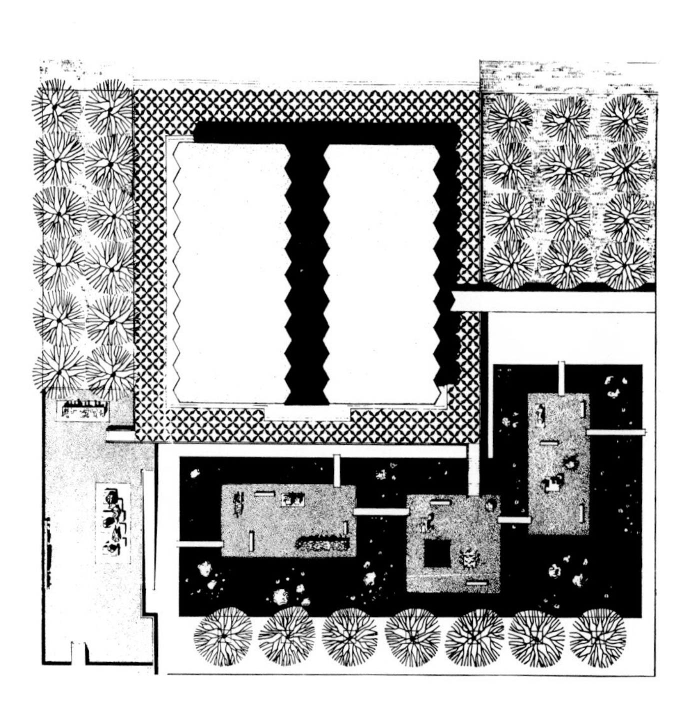

Minoru Yamasaki & Associates

McGregor Memorial Community Conference Center, Detroit, Michigan. 1959 Honor Award. Owner: Wayne State University. Photo: Baltazar Korab.

This building serves as a symbolic gateway to Wayne University. It is a meeting ground between the academic community and the outside. The building contains several meeting rooms of varied size with enough flexibility to accommodate different groups. All meeting rooms open to a skylit two-story lobby. The ornamental quality of the building is derived entirely from its structure. To gain importance, the building is set on a platform surrounded by sunken gardens with pools, rocks, plants, and white gravel islands to serve as exhibit areas for sculpture.

Robert L. Geddes, Melvin Brecher, and Warren W. Cunningham

Moore School of Electrical Engineering, University of Pennsylvania, Philadelphia, Pennsylvania.

1960 Honor Award. Owner: The Moore School of Electrical Engineering.

Photos: Lawrence S. Williams.

The jury was particularly impressed by how well the architects had solved the problem of relating this building to the two adjacent engineering buildings of different scale and character. The well-articulated façade (the view of which is, as so often happens, marred by overhead wiring) displays a fine sense of proportion. The building is constructed on a two-way structural grid of reinforced concrete, and all ducts, lighting, wiring, and other mechanical services are accommodated within that grid. They are flexible and can be readily changed.

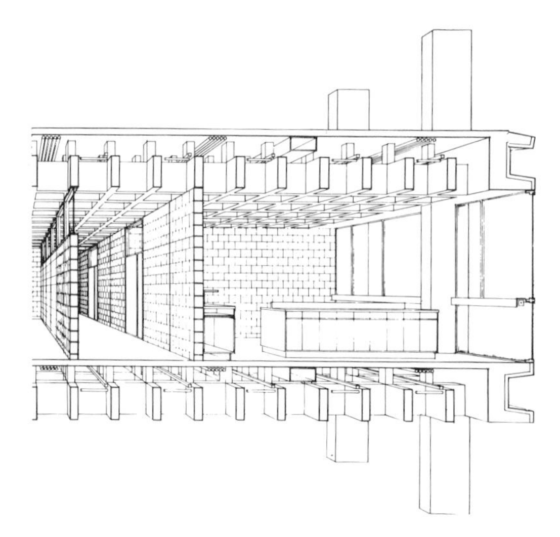

Young, Richardson, Carleton & Detlie

Men's Residence Hall, University of Washington, Seattle, Washington. 1954. Photo: Charles R. Pearson.

Desmond & Davis

Cafeteria Building, Southeastern Louisiana College, Hammond, Louisiana. 1958. Photo: Frank Lotz Miller.

Victor Christ-Janer and Associates

Lincoln Commons Building, Lake Erie College, Painesville, Ohio. 1959. Photo: Robert Stahman.

9

SCHOOLS

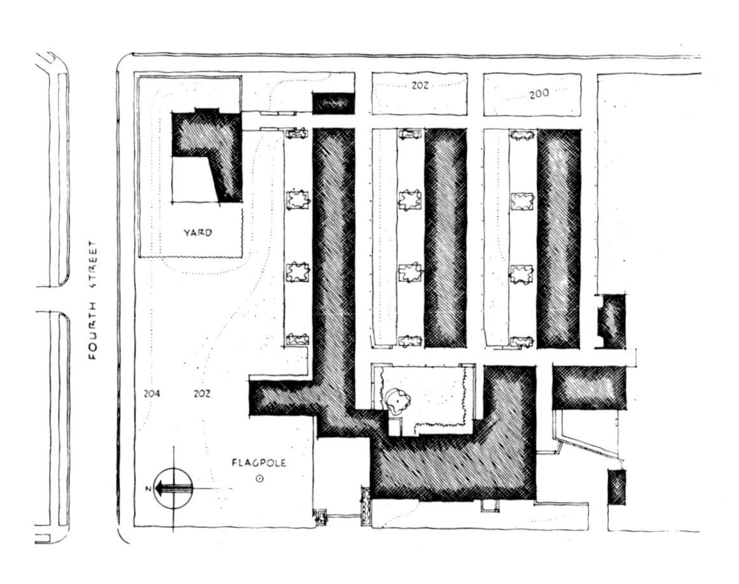
202
200
YARD
FOURTH STREET
204
202
FLAGPOLE
N

Marsh, Smith and Powell

Corona Del Mar Elementary School, Corona Del Mar, California.

1949 Honor Award. Photos: Fred R. Dapprich.

This school was constructed during the war years when construction materials were still scarce. The walls are wood framed and stuccoed, with composition roofing. Located in a residential neighborhood, the design was kept in scale with the adjacent homes. The outstanding feature of this school is its finger plan with delightfully landscaped courts between the one-story classroom wings. The higher entrance unit houses the heating equipment.

O'Dell, Hewlett & Luckenbach Associates

Wing Lake School, Bloomfield Hills, Michigan. 1947. Owner: Board of Education, Bloomfield Hills School District No. 2. Photo: Joe Monroe.

Daniel, Mann, Johnson & Mendenhall

Atascadero Elementary School. Atascadero, California. 1948. Owner: Atascadero School District. Photo: Daniel, Mann, Johnson & Mendenhall.

John Lyon Reid

Fairfax Elementary School. Fairfax, Marin County, California. 1949. Owner: Fairfax Elementary School District. Photo: Roger Sturtevant.

George L. Dahl

Central Elementary School,
Texarkana, Texas. 1949.
Owner: Texarkana Independent
School District.

Perkins & Will

Rugen Elementary School,
Glenview, Illinois. 1946.
Owner: Board of Education,
Consolidated District No. 34.
Photo: Hedrich-Blessing.

Donald Barthelme

St. Rose of Lima School,
Houston, Texas. 1948.
Owner: St. Rose of Lima
Parish. Photo: Donald
Barthelme.

Perkins & Will; Caudill, Rowlett, Scott and Associates, Associated Architects

Norman High School, Norman, Oklahoma. 1954 Honor Award. Owner: Board of Education, Independent School District No. 29, Norman, Oklahoma. Photos: Hedrich-Blessing.

This school was designed as a community center for youth to accommodate fluctuations in enrollment and curriculum. Much thought was given to the details to make it economical both in construction and maintenance. Top lighting through the flat roofs and unobtrusive columns permit moving the interior partitions without loss of illumination. The well-lighted, pleasant main concourse doubles as a student center and is used for exhibits, a lounge, the auditorium lobby, library reading room, locker space, and waiting area for the administrative offices.

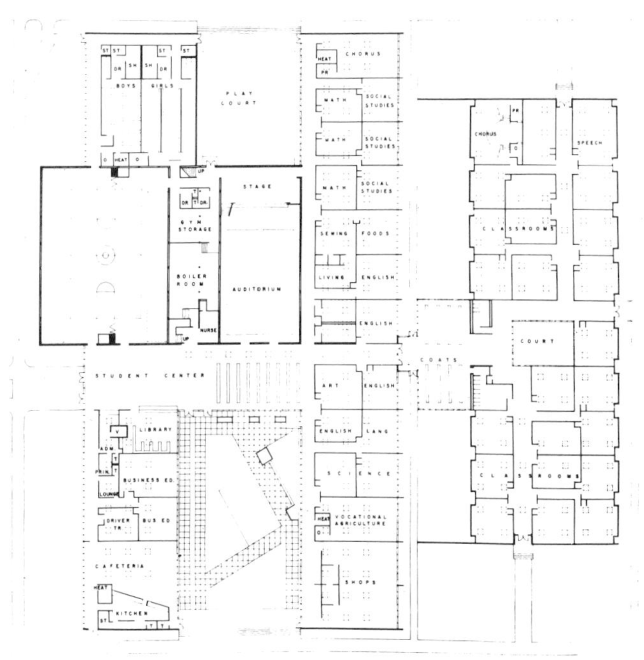

ST
DR
SH
BOYS
GIRLS
PLAY COURT
HEAT
UP
STAGE
GYM STORAGE
BOILER ROOM
NURSE
AUDITORIUM
STUDENT CENTER
LIBRARY
ADM.
PRIN.
LOUNGE
BUSINESS ED.
DRIVER TR.
BUS ED
CAFETERIA
KITCHEN
CHORUS
PR
MATH
SOCIAL STUDIES
SEWING
FOODS
LIVING
ENGLISH
ART
LANG
SCIENCE
VOCATIONAL AGRICULTURE
SHOPS
COATS
SPEECH
CLASSROOMS
COURT

Curtis & Davis

Thomy Lafon School, New Orleans, Louisiana. 1954 Honor Award. Owner: Orleans Parish School Board. Photos: Frank Lotz Miller.

This school is designed for a highly congested slum area with very high land-cost. Only three and one-half acres could be secured, instead of the approximately eight or ten needed to accommodate 525 children and give them the necessary play area and community facilities. Curtis & Davis therefore raised the classroom wing above ground, thus opening the entire first floor to play space some of which is covered. This solution also proved to have the advantage that the classrooms are considerably cooler in the humid Louisiana climate. Direct stairs from the ground to the classrooms eliminate corridors at a substantial saving in construction and maintenance. The community room, library, and auditorium with stage are on the ground level of the main body of the building and adjacent to the street. This makes them available for community use without in any way interfering with the school plant. A brilliant solution wherein "commodity, firmness, and delight" merge to result in substantial economy.

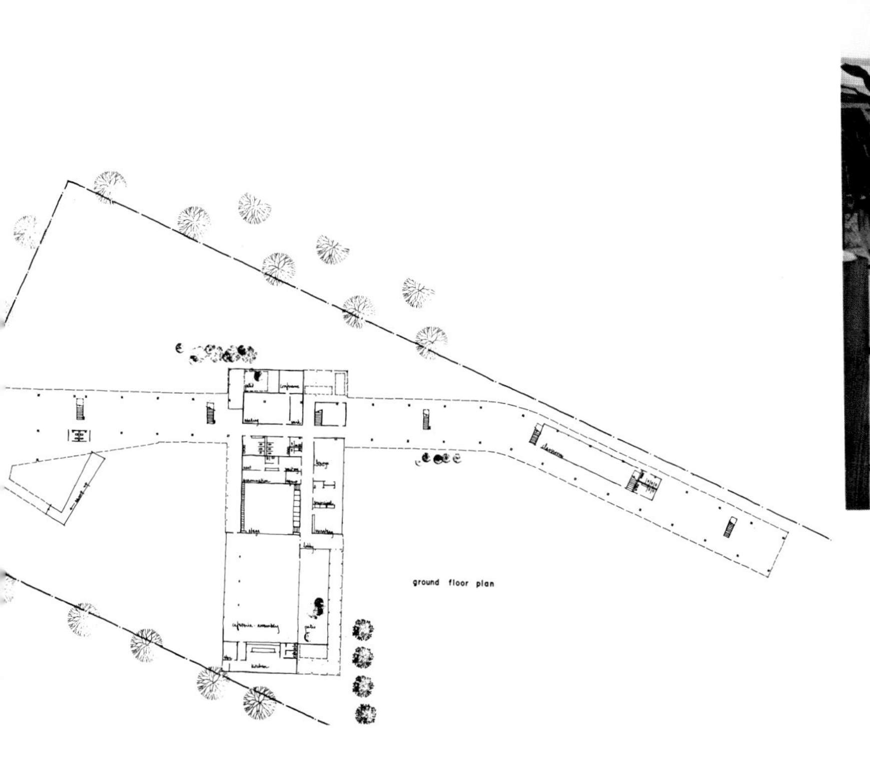
ground floor plan

Maynard Lyndon

Apperson Street School, Los Angeles, California. 1947. Owner: Los Angeles City School District. Photo: Maynard Lyndon.

David H. Horn & Marshall D. Mortland

Sunshine School for the Cerebral Palsied, Fresno, California. Stage 1, 1950; stage 2, 1952. Owner: Fresno City Unified School District. Photo: Julius Shulman.

John Lyon Reid

Manor School, Fairfax, Marin County, California. 1953. Owner: Fairfax Elementary School District. Photo: Roger Sturtevant.

John Carl Warnecke and Associates

White Oaks Elementary School Annex, San Carlos, California. 1953. Owner: San Carlos School District. Photo: Rondal Partridge.

Arthur Gould Odell, Jr.

Double Oaks Elementary School, Charlotte, North Carolina. 1953. Owner: Charlotte City Schools. Photo: Joseph W. Molitor.

John Carl Warnecke and Associates

Mira Vista Elementary School, Richmond, California. 1951. Owner: Richmond Unified Elementary School District. Photo: Rondal Partridge.

John Lyon Reid

Garfield School, Carmichael, Sacramento County, California. 1953. Owner: Arden-Carmichael Elementary School District. Photo: Roger Sturtevant.

Bassetti, Morse and Aitken

Lakeview School, Mercer Island, Washington. 1954. Owner: School District 400, Mercer Island. Photo: Art Hupy.

Curtis & Davis

St. Frances Cabrini School, New Orleans, Louisiana. 1953. Owner: Congregation of St. Frances Cabrini Roman Catholic Church. Photo: Frank Lotz Miller.

Ernest J. Kump, James D. Fessenden, Delp W. Johnson

San Jose High School, San Jose, California. 1952. Owner: San Jose Unified School District. Photo: Roger Sturtevant.

Perkins & Will

Keokuk Senior High School and Community College, Keokuk, Iowa. 1953. Owner: Board of Directors, Independent School District of the City of Keokuk. Photo: Hedrich-Blessing.

Ernest J. Kump

North Hillsborough School, Hillsborough, California. 1955 Honor Award.

Owner: Hillsborough Elementary School District. Photos: Roger Sturtevant.

Kump is known as a pioneer in modern school design with a healthy respect for the natural and human environment of his buildings. Hillsborough, completed in 1950, with additions in 1952 and 1956, shows sympathy for its residential surroundings. It has what the architect calls "a semi-domestic quality desirable in elementary schools." The roofs are pitched, the overhangs wide and sheltering, and the materials rich and warm. All the details are crisp and rhythmic. For flexibility, the steel frame is outside the walls and structurally independent of them and of the interior partitions.

John Lyon Reid & Partners

Hillsdale High School, San Mateo, California. 1956 Honor Award.

Owner: San Mateo Union High School District. Photos: Roger Sturtevant.

The basic design premise of this school in the Miesian manner is that it be flexible—that it shelter with grace the known program of the present, the unknown programs of the future, and the change which secondary education is sure to undergo. The building is therefore designed on a modular plan of natural and artificial illumination, of heating and ventilation, and of room division and arrangement. The partitions can be moved at will and the exterior wall system is so designed that opaque and glass panels can be interchanged. To make the room arrangement independent of window walls, the building has skylights throughout.

Warren H. Ashley

Junior-Senior High School, Greenburgh, New York. 1957 Honor Award.

Owner: Town of Greenburgh, New York. Photos: Joseph W. Molitor.

The architect's task here was to design a school for 550 students, including a gymnasium and a small auditorium, without disrupting a hilly, thickly wooded, and rocky seventy-acre site. The rambling array of structures is of simple steel frame with bar-joist construction walled by glass, porcelain enameled steel panels, and masonry. The roofed walkways connect the various buildings in a pleasant, informal manner.

Skidmore, Owings & Merrill

U. S. Naval Postgraduate School, Monterey, California. 1955. Owner: U. S. Government. Photo: Morley Baer.

Arthur Gould Odell, Jr.

Wilson Junior High School, Charlotte, North Carolina. 1956. Photo: Joseph W. Molitor.

Caudill, Rowlett, Scott and Associates

San Jacinto Elementary School, Liberty, Texas. 1956. Owner: Board of Trustees, Liberty Independent School District. Photo: Ulric Meisel.

R. B. O'Connor and W. H. Kilham, Jr. Philip M. Chu, Associate

Tokeneke Elementary School, Darien, Connecticut. 1956. Owner: Town of Darien, Connecticut.
Photo: Joseph W. Molitor.

Caudill, Rowlett & Scott Max D. Lovett, Associate Architect

San Angelo Central High School, San Angelo, Texas. 1958. Owner: Board of Trustees, San Angelo Independent School District.
Photo: Ulric Meisel.

Minoru Yamasaki & Associates

Benjamin Franklin Junior High School, Wayne, Michigan. 1959.
Photo: Baltazar Korab.

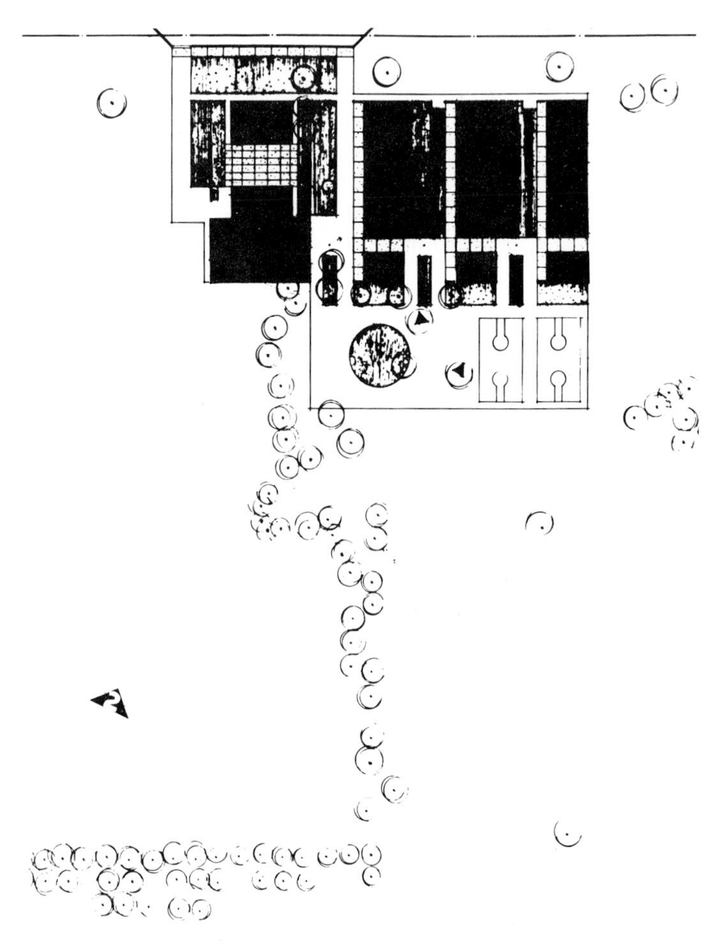

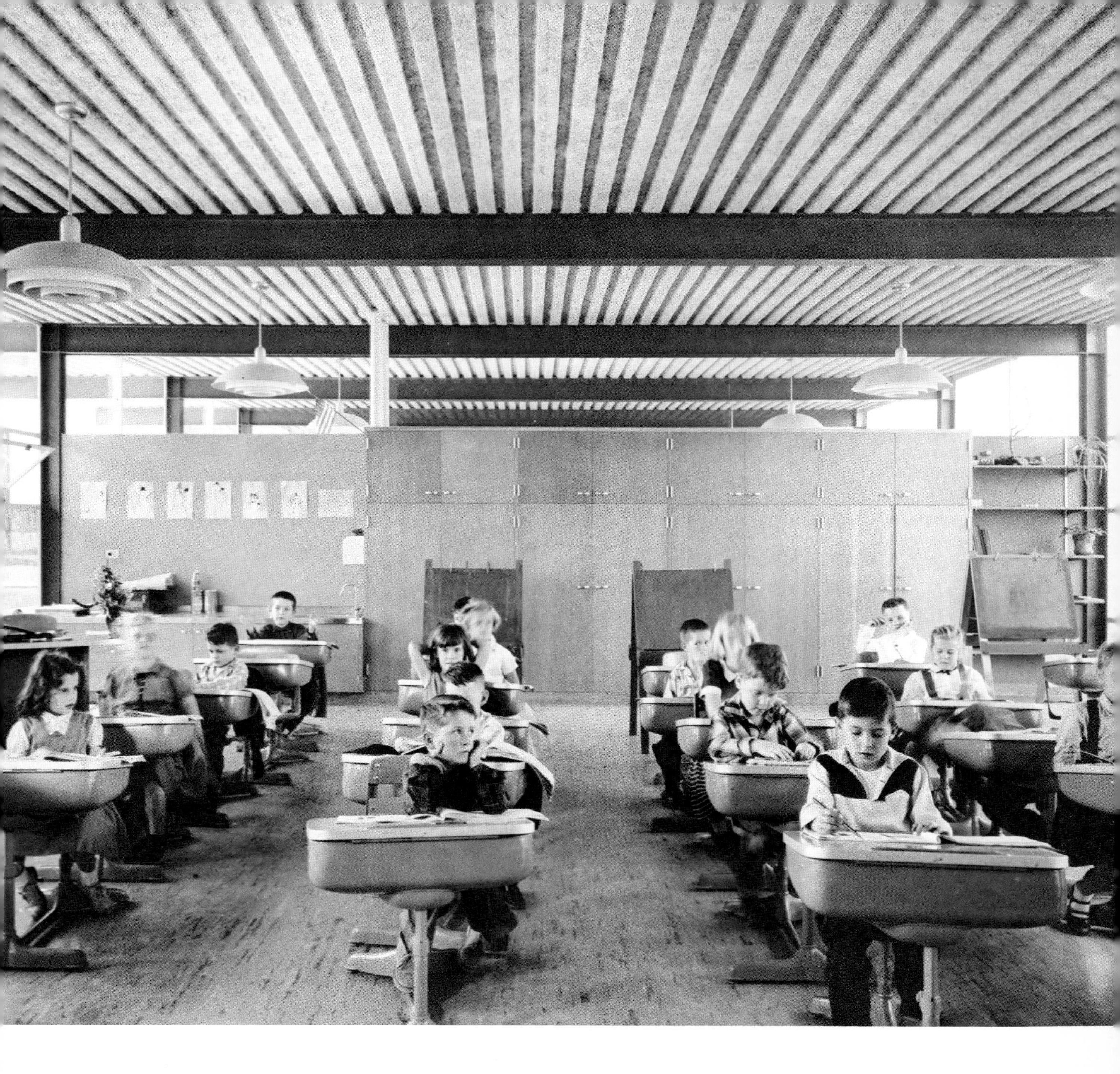

Mario J. Ciampi

Elementary School, Sonoma County, California. 1958 Honor Award.

Owner: Sonoma County School Board. Photos: Rondal Partridge.

One of the requirements the 1958 jury set for itself was the achievement of aesthetic quality by making the structural elements pleasing and decorative. The school has superbly met this requirement—and on a very limited budget. The steel frame, the blown asbestos acoustical ceilings, and even the concrete block end walls have become decorative features. The classrooms are designed for a flexible arrangement of furniture. Free-standing columns were eliminated from the covered corridors to avoid accidents. The landscaping of the level site was done by landscape architect Lawrence Halprin.

Mario J. Ciampi

Westmoor High School, Daly City, California. 1958 Honor Award.

Photos: Karl H. Riek.

This one-story reinforced concrete high school is situated on a hilltop within a quarter-mile of the Pacific Ocean. It is designed to protect the students from the cold off-shore winds and fog by its compact plan and interior rooms and courtyards. The rooms can be easily darkened to show movies and slides. Their partitions are largely glass panels or panels of porcelain enamel in various colors which open one room into the other to avoid a feeling of gloominess. Throughout the complex are landscaped courtyards of varying size and murals and textured walls to brighten the environment.

Mario J. Ciampi
Paul Reiter, Associate

Fernando Rivera Elementary School, Daly City, California. 1961 Honor Award. Owner: Jefferson Elementary School District. Photos: Karl H. Riek.

The children of this twelve-classroom school, complete with its library and other facilities, share a city park with others. With the gay pattern of its folded plywood roof, its colorful wind and vandalism screens, and the free-standing sculpture by Leonard Stanley, it enhances the park. The structural system proved easy to handle and unusually economical. The jury praised "the beautifully articulated plan" and the distinguished use of art which has been utilized "to create a delightful environment."

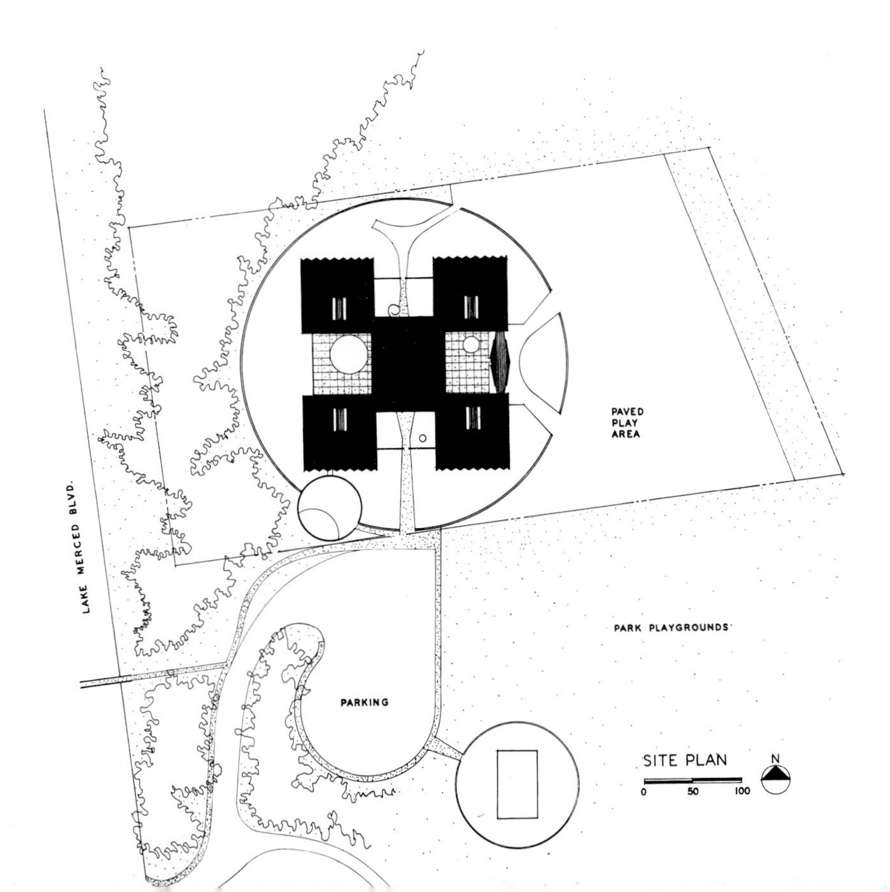

10

RESIDENCES AND APARTMENTS

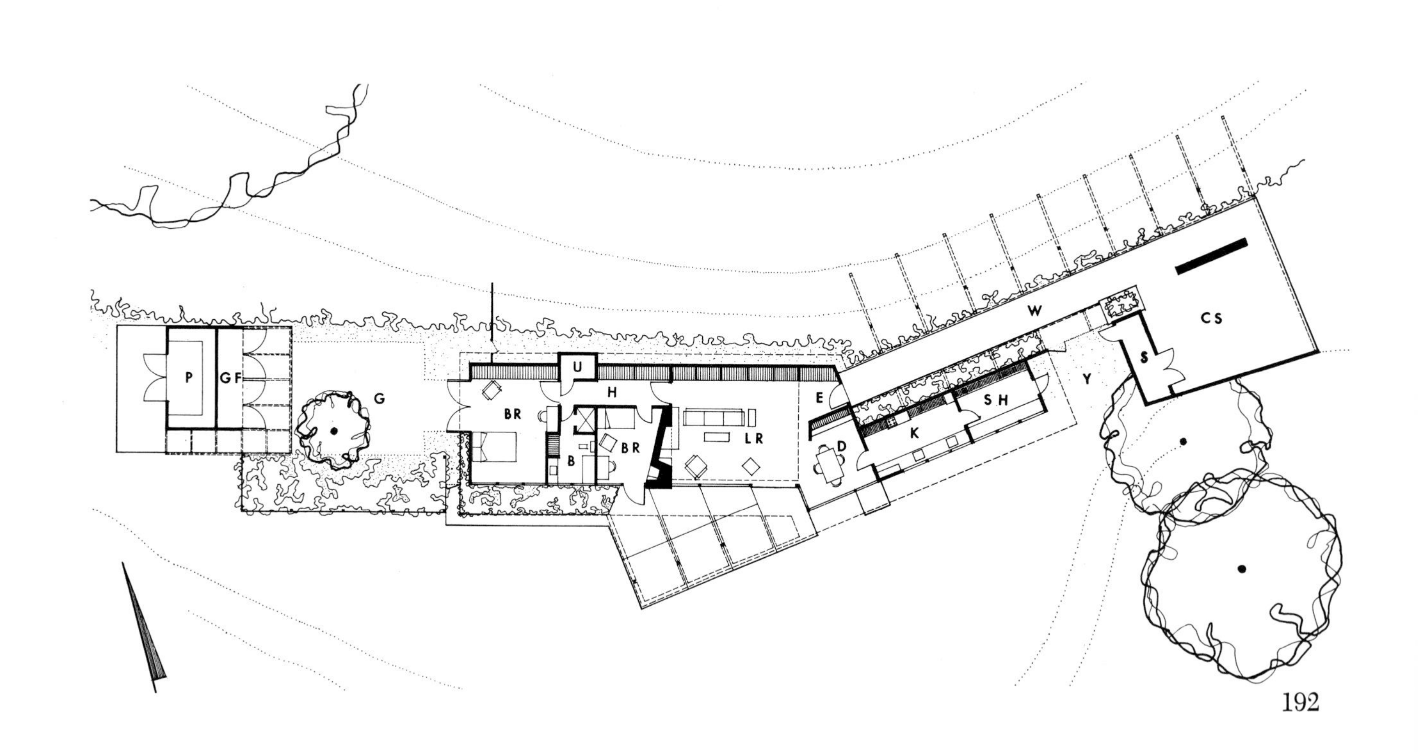

P
GF
G
BR
U
H
BR
B
LR
E
D
K
SH
W
Y
S
CS

Fred Langhorst

Residence for Dr. and Mrs. Alex J. Ker, Marin County, California.

1949 Honor Award. Photos: Roger Sturtevant.

At a time when modern residential design was often criticized for being "nude," "asceptic," or "dull," this house, completed in 1947, showed that the new architecture can be as warm and expressive as anyone could wish. It strings along a steep slope without disturbing the hillside. You enter from the parking space via a covered walk, wedged between the house and the hill. The open living room with its view across the trellised terrace offers a pleasant and hospitable contrast with the confinement of the entrance walk. All rooms of the house are related to a southerly exposure which coincides with the view. All have their appropriate outdoor living area.

Frances E. Lloyd

Residence for John C. Scudder,

Carmel Valley, California. 1947.

Photo: Stone & Steccati.

Wurster, Bernardi & Emmons

Residence for Nelson T. Nowell,

Carmel, California. 1948.

Photo: Roger Sturtevant.

Robert M. Little and William G. Crawford

Residence for Howard Baxter,

Fort Lauderdale, Florida. 1948.

Carl Koch and Associates

Prefabricated House, Concord, Massachusetts. 1948. Owner: John Bemis. Photo: Ezra Stoller.

Arthur T. Brown

Residence for Mr. and Mrs. L. B. Clothier, Tucson, Arizona. 1947. Photo: Western Ways by Kenneth McVey.

Thornton M. Abell

Residence for Lester H. Wilcox, San Gabriel, California. 1948. Photo: Herman V. Wall.

A. Quincy Jones

Residence of H. C. Hvistendahl, San Diego, California. 1950 Honor Award. Photo: Robert C. Cleveland.

This is a low-cost house on a 1,000 square-foot lot designed for development building. In a minimum 25′ x 40′ rectangle, the illusion of a much larger house has been created by an open plan and walls which are 65 per cent glass. Through these glass walls each of the main rooms is extended into an outdoor garden room, enclosed by fences which assure complete privacy. The solid end walls of the house are topped by a 16-inch band of glass with sliding panels which provide added ventilation. As a result, the roof seems to float lightly over the house.

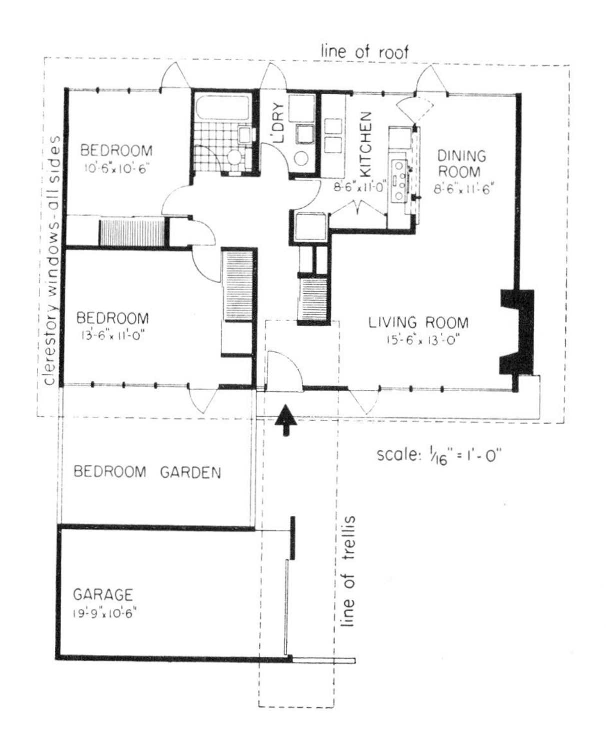

L. Morgan Yost

Residence for Mr. and Mrs. Norman C. Deno, Highland Park, Illinois. 1946. Photo: Nowell Ward.

Mario Francis Corbett

Residence for Mr. and Mrs. Mario Corbett, Wolfback Ridge, Sausalito, California. 1947. Photo: Hal McIntyre.

Twitchell & Rudolph

Residence for Roberta Finney, Sarasota, Florida. 1950. Photo: Ezra Stoller.

Mario F. Corbett

Residence for William Crocker, Wolfback Ridge, Sausalito, California. 1948. Photo: Ernest Braun.

Hugh A. Stubbins, Jr.

Residence for Mrs. Harold Adams, Concord, Massachusetts. 1947. Photo: Ezra Stoller.

Cocke, Bowman & York

Residence for W. B. Uhlhorn, Harlingen, Texas. 1951. Photo: Purnell Photographers.

Raphael S. Soriano

Residence for Allan Olds, Los Angeles, California. 1950. For *Arts & Architecture Magazine* Case Study House, 1950. Photo: James H. Reed.

Maynard Lyndon

Residence for Maynard Lyndon, Malibu, California, 1949. Photo: Maynard Lyndon.

Sherlock, Smith & Adams

Residence for Mr. and Mrs. Fred M. Lyon, Mary Esther, Florida. 1950. Photo: Scott Photographic Services—Betty Baldwin.

Anshen & Allen

Residence for Mrs. Sonya Silverstone, Taxco, Mexico. 1949. Photo: Maynard L. Parker.

Alexander S. Cochran

Residence for Alexander S. Cochran, Baltimore, Maryland. 1951. Photo: Alexander Cochran.

Richard J. Neutra

Residence for Dr. and Mrs. Stuart G. Bailey, Pacific Palisades, California. 1948. Photo: Julius Shulman.

Mario F. Corbett

Residence for Moritz Thomsen, Vina, California. 1950. Photo: Stone & Steccati.

Edward A. Killingsworth

Office/Residence for Mr. and Mrs. John E. Baird, Los Alamitos, California. 1951. Photo: Marvin Rand.

Whitney R. Smith, A. Quincy Jones, Edgardo Contini

500 Home Community, Brentwood, California. 1951. Owner: Mutual Housing Association. Photo: Julius Shulman.

Richard J. Neutra

Residence for Mr. and Mrs. J. C. O'Brien, Shreveport, Louisiana. 1951.

Richard J. Neutra

Residence for Mr. and Mrs. J. D. Hinds, Los Angeles, California. 1951. Photo: Julius Shulman.

Bassetti & Morse

Residence for Mr. and Mrs. Marshall Forrest, Bellingham, Washington. 1952. Photo: Dearborn-Massar.

Richard Neutra

Residence of Mr. and Mrs. James D. Moore, Jr., Ojai, California.

1954 Honor Award. Photos: Julius Shulman.

Neutra, who ranks among the great architects of our time, has designed all types of buildings. But in none of them, he says, "does an architect gain so much clinical experience, as a doctor would call it, as when he sees the members of a family for which he designs a house and makes physical arrangements for a long future ahead." The Moore family settled in Ojai valley for its natural beauty, mild climate, and cultural stimulation. Their residence consists of a main house and, connected with it by stone stairs and vine overgrown pergola, a studio and guest house. The living area relates intimately to the stone pier which juts out into the waters of the cooling pond, providing a pleasant outside sitting space. The pond also serves as an irrigation pool and refreshes the profuse planting of the slopes to which the building group is organically attached.

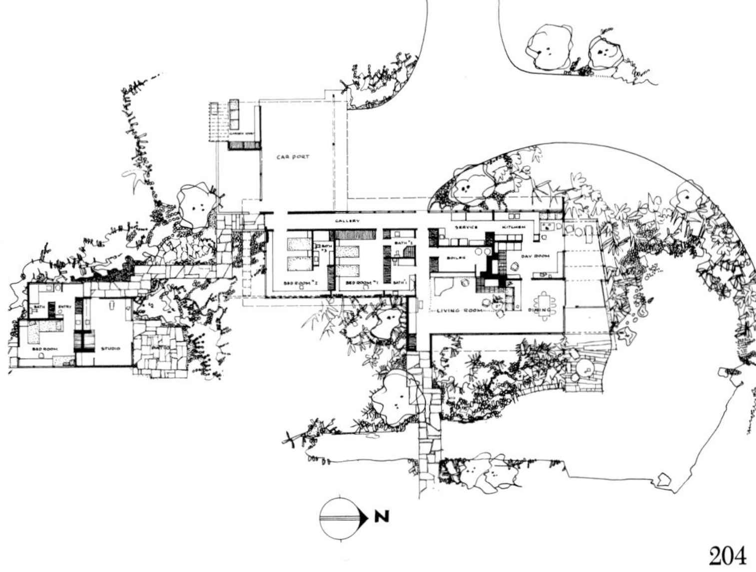

Anshen & Allen

Development House, Santa Clara, California. 1953. Owner: Mr. and Mrs. Joseph De Jesus. Photo: Roger Sturtevant.

Anshen & Allen

Sunshine Glen, Palo Alto, California. 1954. Owner: Mr. and Mrs. Frank D. Paone. Photo: Mason Weymouth.

Anshen & Allen

Sunshine Meadows, Santa Clara, California. 1954. Photo: Roger Sturtevant.

Carl Koch

Techbuilt House, Weston, Massachusetts. 1953. Owner: Techbuilt, Inc. Photo: Ben Schnall.

George Vernon Russell

Residence for John J. Pike, Los Angeles, California. 1951. Photo: Ernest Braun.

Smith and Williams

Blue Ribbon Tract, Reseda, California. 1953. Owner: Blue Ribbon Construction Co. Photo: Julius Shulman.

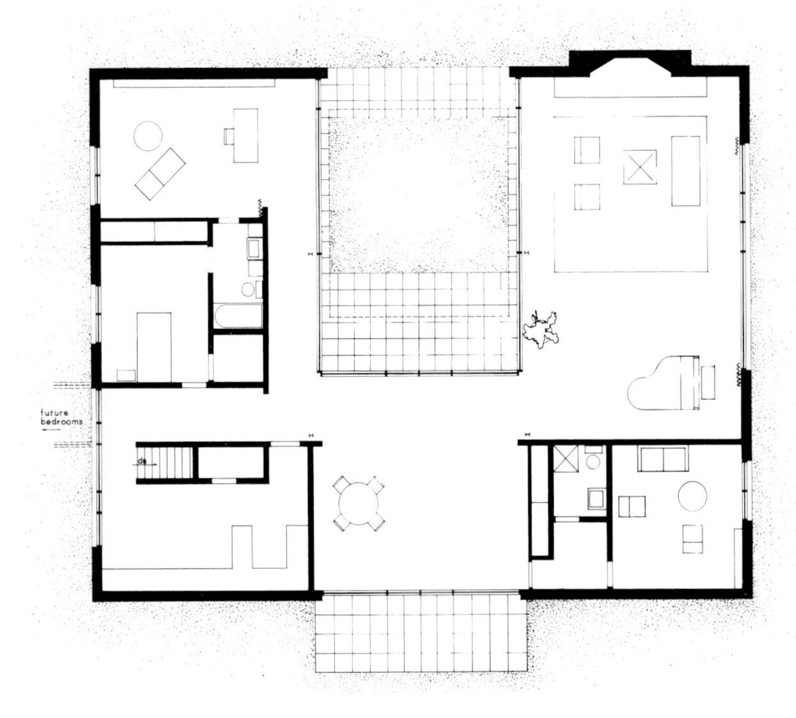
future
bedrooms

Philip C. Johnson

Residence for Mr. and Mrs. Richard Hodgson, New Canaan, Connecticut.

1956 Honor Award. Photos: Ezra Stoller.

An echo of Mies van der Rohe's famous Farnsworth House of 1950 at Plano, Illinois, this symmetrical residence frames an interior patio full of foliage. Living, sleeping, and service areas are separated for privacy but not harshly segregated. As in Mies' work, the splendor of this building results from the refinement of its details and the measured perfection of its proportions.

Bassetti & Morse

Residence for Mr. and Mrs. Gerald Martin, Seattle, Washington. 1953. Photo: Art Hupy.

Roger Lee

Residence for Mr. and Mrs. George Channing, Sausalito, California. 1953. Photo: Ernest Braun.

Charles M. Goodman

Residence for Mr. and Mrs. Alex Radin, Hollin Hills, Alexandria, Virginia. 1954. Photo: Robert C. Lautman.

Anshen & Allen

Beach House for Dr. and Mrs. Ernest N. Moore, Yankee Point, Carmel, California. 1953. Photo: George Cain.

George Fred Keck—William Keck

Residence for Sigmund Kunstadter, Highland Park, Illinois. 1952. Photo: Hedrich-Blessing.

Charles M. Goodman

Residence for Mr. and Mrs. Charles M. Goodman, Alexandria, Virginia. 1955. Photo: Robert C. Lautman.

Eliot Noyes

Eliot Noyes House, New Canaan, Connecticut. 1957 Honor Award.

Photos: Ezra Stoller.

The house this architect-industrial designer built for himself in 1955 seems to prove two things: first, a simple, unadorned design can be warm and decorative; and second, the indoor-outdoor relationship need not be confined to the benign climate of California. Between its rustic fieldstone walls, which almost camouflage the house in its woodland setting, are two rectangular elements separated by an interior court. One contains the study, living-dining area, and kitchen. The other contains five bedrooms. At the center of each of the stone walls are large sliding doors which can open the court to the surrounding site or may be closed for complete privacy. Steel columns span the enclosure between the walls.

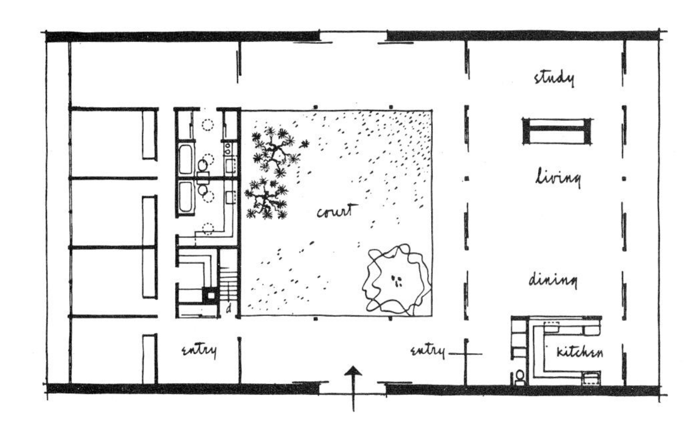

Raphael S. Soriano

Residence for Mr. and Mrs. Edwin Krause, Whittier, California. 1952. Photo: Julius Shulman.

Jasper D. Ward
Reginald Caywood Knight

Residence for Mr. and Mrs. Walter P. Swain, Jr., Plainfield, New Jersey. 1952. Photo: Garrett Jupp.

Wurster, Bernardi & Emmons

Residence for Mr. and Mrs. Theodore Bernardi, Sausalito, California. 1951. Photo: Ernest Braun. Courtesy *Sunset Magazine.*

George Matsumoto

Residence-Studio, Raleigh, North Carolina. 1954. Owner: George and Kimi Matsumoto. Photo: Joseph W. Molitor.

Edward B. Page

Residence for Mason B. Wells, Belvedere, California. 1954. Photo: Edward B. Page.

A. Quincy Jones and Frederick E. Emmons

Residence for Mr. and Mrs. Frederick E. Emmons, Pacific Palisades, California. 1955. Photo: Julius Shulman.

Wurster, Bernardi & Emmons

Residence for Mr. and Mrs. Nelson T. Nowell, Stockton, California. 1956. Photo: Roger Sturtevant.

Thornton Ladd

Studio at Pasadena, California. 1950. Owner: Thornton Ladd, Photo: Irving Kershner.

A. Quincy Jones and Frederick E. Emmons

Residence for Mr. and Mrs. A. Quincy Jones, Los Angeles, California. 1955. Photo: Julius Shulman.

George T. Rockrise

Residence for Mr. and Mrs. Dunbar Carpenter, Medford, Oregon. 1955. Photo: Ernest Braun. Courtesy *Sunset Magazine*.

John Black Lee

Residence for Mr. and Mrs. John Black Lee, New Canaan, Connecticut. 1956. Photo: Joseph W. Molitor.

Ulrich Franzen

Residence for Mr. and Mrs. Richard Beattie, Rye, New York. 1958. Photo: Ezra Stoller.

John Carl Warnecke & Associates

Asilomar Housing, Pacific Grove, California. 1959. Owner: Pacific Grove-Asilomar Operating Company. Photo: Roger Sturtevant.

Richard Dorman & Associates

Residence for Mr. and Mrs. Neil Lakenan, Beverly Hills, California. 1956. Photo: George de Gennaro.

Lee Stuart Darrow

Residence for Alyn B. Reid, Mill Valley, California. 1957. Photo: Ernest Braun. Courtesy *Sunset Magazine.*

Killingsworth, Brady and Smith

Residence for Mr. and Mrs. Richard Opdahl, Long Beach, California. 1960 Honor Award. Photos: Marvin Rand.

Here is an outstanding example of the flowing outdoor-indoor relationship and the emphasis on unpretentious privacy in modern home design. It was accomplished against the odds of an extremely narrow site, wedged between an old apartment house (left) and a one and one-half story residence (right). The two-story living room in the front of the house merges (through a glass wall) with a well-sheltered patio and reflection pool. There are two bedrooms upstairs and the structure allows for expansion. The rear wall is also of glass, affording a glimpse of the bay.

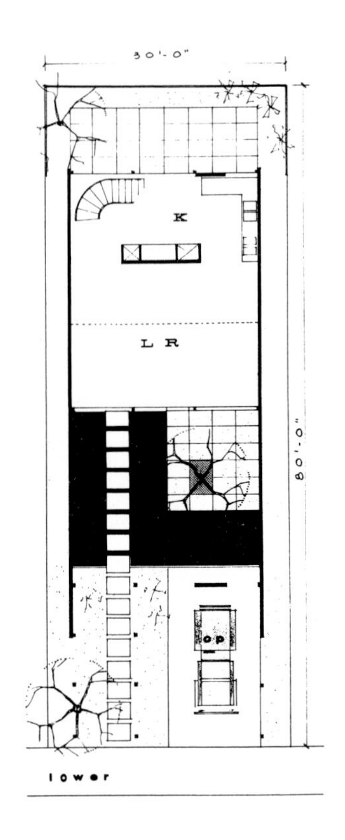

Birkerts & Straub

Summer House for Mr. and Mrs. Alan Schwartz, Northville, Michigan. 1961 Honor Award.

Photos: Baltazar Korab.

Designed by two young architects, this compact four-bedroom house opens all around onto its unusual setting—a huge apple orchard. Yet, for all its glass walls, it gives its owners a feeling of solid security. The forceful, predominantly horizontal rectangles are accentuated by the bold tube of the chimney. The interior organization is simplicity itself: It puts the kitchen and utilities into the central core and clearly separates the private bedroom area from the living-dining room by the two baths. The traffic moves around the central core. Three square stepping-stone slabs echo the sun porch and, set off to the side, accent the symmetry of the composition.

Raphael S. Soriano

Builder's House, Mill Valley, California. 1949. Photo: Ken Knolenberg. Courtesy Bethlehem Steel Co.

Charles R. Colbert of Colbert, Lowrey, Hess, Boudreaux

Residence for Dr. Henry G. Simon, New Orleans, Louisiana. 1960. Photo: Frank Lotz Miller.

William Hoskins Brown, Vernon De Mars, Robert Woods Kennedy, Carl Koch, Ralph Rapson

100 Memorial Drive Apartments, Cambridge, Massachusetts. 1950. Photo: Ezra Stoller.

Keyes, Smith, Satterlee & Lethbridge

Apartment Development, Fairfax County, Virginia. 1955. Photo: Robert C. Lautman.

Carl L. Maston

Five Unit Apartment Building, Los Angeles, California. 1954. Owner: Carl Maston. Photo: Julius Shulman.

Ralph Rapson and John Van Der Meulen

U. S. Embassy Staff Apartments, Paris, France. 1955. Owner: U. S. State Department. Photo: Ralph Rapson.

Satterlee & Smith

The Capitol Park Apartments, Washington, D. C. 1960. Owners: Roger L. Stevens and James H. Scheuer. Photo: Ezra Stoller.

Meathe, Kessler & Associates, Inc.

Clemens Homes PHA Project (Mich. 28-1), Mount Clemens, Michigan. 1959. Owner: Mount Clemens Public Housing Commission. Photo: Baltazar Korab.

John Carl Warnecke and Associates

Willow Creek Apartments, Palo Alto, California. 1960. Owner: Willow Creek Corporation. Photo: Roger Sturtevant.

CHRONOLOGICAL LISTING OF AWARDS

1949

FIRST HONOR AWARDS

Corona Del Mar Elementary School, Corona Del Mar, Calif.; Marsh, Smith and Powell
Residence, Dr. and Mrs. Alex J. Ker, Marin County, Calif., Fred Langhorst

AWARDS OF MERIT

Fairfax Elementary School, Fairfax, Calif.; John Lyon Reid
Apperson Street School, Los Angeles, Calif.; Maynard Lyndon
Atascadero Elementary School, Atascadero, Calif.; Daniel, Mann, Johnson & Mendenhall
Rugen Elementary School, Glenview, Ill.; Perkins & Will
Wing Lake School, Bloomfield Hills, Mich.; O'Dell, Hewlett & Luckenback Associates
St. Rose of Lima School, Houston, Tex.; Donald Barthelme
Central Elementary School, Texarkana, Tex.; George L. Dahl
Residence, Nelson T. Nowell, Carmel, Calif.; Wurster, Bernardi & Emmons
Residence, Lester H. Wilcox, San Gabriel, Calif.; Thornton M. Abell
Residence, Howard Baxter, Fort Lauderdale, Fla.; Robert M. Little; William G. Crawford
Residence, Mr. and Mrs. Mario Corbett, Sausalito, Calif.; Mario Francis Corbett
Residence, John C. Scudder, Carmel Valley, Calif.; Frances E. Lloyd
Residence, Mr. and Mrs. Norman C. Deno, Highland Park, Ill.; L. Morgan Yost
Residence, Mr. and Mrs. L. B. Clothier, Tucson, Ariz.; Arthur T. Brown
Prefabricated House, Concord, Mass.; Carl Koch and Associates

1950

FIRST HONOR AWARDS

Residence, H. C. Hvistendahl, San Diego, Calif.; A. Quincy Jones
Davison-Paxon Company Store, Atlanta, Ga.; Harold M. Heatley; Ketchum, Gina & Sharp

AWARDS OF MERIT

Residence, William Crocker, Sausalito, Calif.; Mario F. Corbett
Residence, Mrs. Harold Adams, Concord, Mass.; Hugh A. Stubbins, Jr.
Residence, Roberta Finney, Sarasota, Fla.; Twitchell & Rudolph
Wallachs Clothing Store, Jamaica, N. Y.; Ketchum, Gina & Sharp

Bercu Pipe Shop, Los Angeles, Calif.; Welton D. Becket
Bullock's, Pasadena, Calif.; Welton D. Becket
Santa Fe City Ticket Office, Los Angeles, Calif.; Maynard Lyndon
Foley's Department Store, Houston, Tex.; Kenneth Franzheim

1951

FIRST HONOR AWARDS

Clearwater County Memorial Hospital, Bagley, Minn.; Thorshov & Cerny
Coca-Cola Bottling Plant, Houston, Tex.; Stone & Pitts

AWARDS OF MERIT

Residence, Mrs. Sonya Silverstone, Taxco, Mexico; Anshen & Allen
Residence, W. B. Uhlhorn, Harlingen, Tex.; Cocke, Bowman & York
Residence, Alexander S. Cochran, Baltimore, Md.; Alexander S. Cochran
Residence, Maynard Lyndon, Malibu, Calif.; Maynard Lyndon
Residence, Dr. and Mrs. Stuart G. Bailey, Pacific Palisades, Calif.; Richard J. Neutra
Residence, Mr. and Mrs. Fred M. Lyon, Mary Esther, Fla.; Sherlock, Smith & Adams
Residence, Allan Olds, Los Angeles, Calif.; Raphael S. Soriano
Residence, Mr. and Mrs. Isadore Schuman, Woodside, Calif.; Wurster, Bernardi & Emmons
Northern Indiana Hospital for Crippled Children, South Bend, Ind.; Pohlmeyer & Pohlmeyer; Skidmore, Owings & Merrill
Georgia Baptist Hospital, Atlanta, Ga.; Stevens & Wilkinson
Perry County Hospital, Marion, Ala.; Sherlock, Smith & Adams
Goodyear Memorial Pavilion, Ventura, Calif.; Allison and Rible
Xavier Hospital, Dubuque, Iowa; Schmidt, Garden & Erikson
St. Frances Cabrini Hospital, Alexandria, La.; Golemon & Rolfe
U. S. Veterans Administration Hospital, Wilkes-Barre, Pa.; Kelly & Gruzen; Isadore Rosenfield
U. S. Veterans Administration Hospital, Fort Wayne, Ind.; Giffels & Vallet, Inc.; A. M. Strauss
Electronics Plant, San Carlos, Calif.; Francis Joseph McCarthy

1952

FIRST HONOR AWARDS

Lever House, New York, N. Y.; Skidmore, Owings & Merrill
William S. Beckett's Office, Los Angeles, Calif.; William S. Beckett
Gaffney's Lake Wilderness, Maple Valley, Wash.; Young, Richardson, Carleton & Detlie

AWARDS OF MERIT

Residence, Moritz Thomsen, Vina, Calif.; Mario F. Corbett
Apartment House, 100 Memorial Drive, Cambridge, Mass; William Hoskins Brown; Vernon De Mars; Robert Woods Kennedy; Carl Koch; Ralph Rapson
Cerebral Palsy School, Fresno, Calif.; David H. Horn, Marshall D. Mortland
Pontchartrain Beach Bus Shelter, New Orleans, La.; Freret & Wolf
Illinois Children's Home & Aid Society, Chicago, Ill.; Skidmore, Owings & Merrill
500 Home Community, Brentwood, Calif.; Whitney R. Smith; A. Quincy Jones; Edgardo Contini
Insurance Office Building, Los Angeles, Calif.; Richard J. Neutra
Residence, Mr. and Mrs. J. D. Hinds, Los Angeles, Calif.; Richard J. Neutra
Office/Residence, Mr. and Mrs. John E. Baird, Los Alamitos, Calif.; Edward A. Killingsworth
Residence, Mr. and Mrs. J. C. O'Brien, Shreveport, La.; Richard J. Neutra

1953

FIRST HONOR AWARDS

Engineering Staff Buildings, General Motors Technical Center, Warren, Mich.; Eero Saarinen & Associates
North Carolina State Fair Pavilion, Raleigh, N. C.; William Henley Deitrick

AWARDS OF MERIT

Development House, Santa Clara, Calif.; Anshen & Allen
Corning Glass Center, Corning, N. Y.; Harrison, Abramovitz & Abbe

Offices and Plant, Republic Supply Company, San Leandro, Calif.; George Vernon Russell
Residence, Mr. and Mrs. Marshall Forrest, Bellingham, Wash.; Bassetti & Morse
Residence, Kent Woods, Marin County, Calif.; George T. Rockrise

1954

FIRST HONOR AWARDS

Residence, Mr. and Mrs. James D. Moore, Jr., Ojai, Calif.; Richard Neutra
Lankenau Hospital, Philadelphia, Pa.; Vincent G. Kling
Fort Brown Memorial Civic Center, Brownsville, Tex.; John P. Wiltshire and J. Herschel Fisher
Thomy Lafon School, New Orleans, La.; Curtis & Davis
Norman High School, Norman, Okla.; Perkins & Will; Caudill, Rowlett, Scott and Associates
Santa Monica City College, Santa Monica, Calif.; Smith, Powell & Morgridge

AWARDS OF MERIT

Blue Ribbon Tract, Reseda, Calif.; Smith and Williams
Sunshine Meadows, Santa Clara, Calif.; Anshen & Allen
Residence, Mr. and Mrs. Alex Radin, Hollins Hills, Alexandria, Va.; Charles M. Goodman
Residence, Mr. and Mrs. Gerald Martin, Seattle, Wash.; Bassetti & Morse
Residence, John J. Pike, Los Angeles, Calif.; George Vernon Russell
Mira Vista Elementary School, Richmond, Calif.; John Carl Warnecke and Associates
White Oaks Elementary School Annex, San Carlos, Calif.; John Carl Warnecke and Associates
San Jose High School, San Jose, Calif.; Ernest J. Kump; James D. Fessenden; Delp W. Johnson
Manor School, Fairfax, Marin County, Calif.; John Lyon Reid
Sunshine Glen, Palo Alto, Calif.; Anshen & Allen
Techbuilt House, Weston, Mass.; Carl Koch
Double Oaks Elementary School, Charlotte, N. C.; Arthur Gould Odell, Jr.
Garfield School, Carmichael, Sacramento County, Calif.; John Lyon Reid
St. Frances Xavier Cabrini School, New Orleans, La.; Curtis & Davis
Keokuk Senior High School and Community College, Keokuk, Iowa; Perkins & Will
Lakeview School, Mercer Island, Wash.; Bassetti, Morse and Aitken
Sawyer Biscuit Company Plant, Melrose Park, Ill.; Skidmore, Owings & Merrill
Children's Chapel, Neighborhood Church, Pasadena, Calif.; Smith and Williams
First Church of Christ, Scientist, Victoria, Tex.; Milton A. Ryan
Biochemistry and Virus Laboratory, Berkeley, Calif.; Michael Goodman
Business Education Building, Orange Coast College, Costa Mesa, Calif.; Neutra and Alexander
St. Vincent's Home for the Aged, Omaha, Nebr.; Steele, Sandham & Steele; Alex Weinstein
Peninsula Memorial Blood Bank, Burlingame, San Mateo County, Calif.; Stone & Mulloy; Marraccini and Patterson
CBS Television City, Los Angeles, Calif.; Pereira & Luckman
Refuse Incinerator, Town of Brookline, Mass.; Isidor Richmond and Carney Goldberg
Northland Regional Shopping Center, Southfield Township, Wayne County, Mich.; Victor D. Gruen
Pi Kappa Alpha Fraternity House, Austin, Tex.; Lundgren & Maurer
National Bureau of Standards, Boulder Laboratories, Boulder, Colo.; Pereira & Luckman; J. E. Stanton; Robert W. Ditzen
Apple Valley Inn, Apple Valley, Calif.; G. A. Downs
First Federal Savings and Loan Association of Denver, Denver, Colo.; William C. Muchow Associates
Standard Federal Savings and Loan Association, Los Angeles, Calif.; Wilton Becket and Associates
Girl Scout Lodge, Camp Woodlands, Annapolis, Md.; Rogers, Taliaferro & Lamb

1955

FIRST HONOR AWARDS

North Hillsborough School, Hillsborough, Calif.; Ernest J. Kump
Central Restaurant Building, General Motors Technical Center, Warren, Mich.; Eero Saarinen & Associates
Women's Dormitories and Dining Hall, Drake University, Des Moines, Iowa; Eero Saarinen & Associates

The General Telephone Company of the Southwest, San Angelo, Tex.; Pace Associates

U. S. Embassy, Stockholm, Sweden; Ralph Rapson; John Van Der Meulen

AWARDS OF MERIT

St. Matthews Church, Pacific Palisades, Calif.; A. Quincy Jones; Frederick E. Emmons

Children's Clinic, Raceland, La.; Curtis & Davis

Residence, Sigmund Kunstadter, Highland Park, Ill.; George Fred Keck, William Keck

Apartment Development, Fairfax County, Va.; Keyes, Smith, Satterlee & Lethbridge

Manresa Jesuit Retreat House, Azusa, Calif.; Wallace Neff

Beach House at Yankee Point, Carmel, Calif.; Anshen & Allen

Five Unit Apartment Building, Los Angeles, Calif.; Carl L. Maston

U. S. Naval Postgraduate School, Monterey, Calif.; Skidmore, Owings & Merrill

Mercantile Library, Philadelphia, Pa.: Martin, Stewart & Noble

Residence, Mr. and Mrs. Charles M. Goodman, Alexandria, Va.; Charles M. Goodman

The William H. & May D. Taylor Memorial Library and the John M. Reeves Student Building, Hackettstown, N. J.; Jan Hird Pokorny

O'Neil Sheffield Shopping Center, Sheffield Township, Ohio; Weinberg & Teare

Danforth Chapel, Colorado A. & M. College, Fort Collins, Colo.; James M. Hunter

Bank of Apple Valley, Apple Valley, Calif.; McFarland, Bonsall & Thomas

Men's Residence Hall, University of Washington, Seattle, Wash.; Young, Richardson, Carleton & Detlie

Eagle Rock Playground Club House, Eagle Rock, Calif.; Richard J. Neutra; Dion Neutra

Texas Children's Hospital, Texas Medical Center, Houston, Tex.; Milton Foy Martin

Residence, Mr. and Mrs. George Channing, Sausalito, Calif.; Roger Lee

Home Economics Building, University of California, Davis, Calif.; Clark and Beuttler

Bandstand and Park Pavilion, St. Petersburg, Fla.; William B. Harvard

Service Schools, Great Lakes, Ill.; Skidmore, Owings & Merrill

St. Brigid Catholic Church, Los Angeles, Calif.; Chaix & Johnson

1956

FIRST HONOR AWARDS

Hillsdale High School, San Mateo Union High School District, San Mateo, Calif.; John Lyon Reid & Partners

Center for Advanced Study in Behavioral Sciences, Inc., Stanford University Grounds, Palo Alto, Calif.; Wurster, Bernardi & Emmons

Lambert–St. Louis Municipal Airport Terminal Building, St. Louis, Mo.; Hellmuth, Yamasaki & Leinweber

Manufacturer's Trust Company Fifth Avenue Branch, New York, N. Y.; Skidmore, Owings & Merrill

The Hodgson House, New Canaan, Conn.; Philip C. Johnson

AWARDS OF MERIT

Oak Cliff Savings & Loan Association, Dallas, Tex.; Prinz & Brooks

U. S. Embassy Staff Apartments, Paris, France; Ralph Rapson; John Van Der Meulen

Architect's Office, Long Beach, Calif.; Killingsworth, Brady and Smith

Residence, Mr. and Mrs. Nelson T. Nowell, Stockton, Calif.; Wurster, Bernardi & Emmons

Residence, Mr. and Mrs. Theodore Bernardi, Sausalito, Calif.; Wurster, Bernardi & Emmons

Interfaith Center, Brandeis University, Waltham, Mass.; Harrison & Abramovitz

Residence, Mr. and Mrs. Edwin Krause, Whittier, Calif.; Raphael S. Soriano

Feld Clinic, Detroit, Mich.; Yamasaki, Leinweber and Associates

Hilton Istanbul Hotel, Istanbul, Turkey; Skidmore, Owings & Merrill

First Methodist Church, Midland, Mich.; Alden B. Dow

Police Facilities Building, Civic Center, Los Angeles, Calif.; Welton Becket and Associates; J. E. Stanton

Schlumberger Administration Building, Ridgefield, Conn.; Philip C. Johnson

Mark Thomas Inn, Del Monte, Monterey, Calif.; John Carl Warnecke

Residence, Mr. and Mrs. Walter P. Swain, Jr., Plainfield, N. J.; Jasper D. Ward; Reginald Caywood Knight

1957

FIRST HONOR AWARDS

Office Building for Middlesex Mutual Building Trust, Waltham, Mass.; Anderson, Beckwith and Haible

Junior-Senior High School, Greenburgh, N. Y.; Warren H. Ashley

Eliot Noyes House, New Canaan, Conn.; Eliot Noyes

Brazos County Courthouse and Jail, Bryan, Tex.; Caudill, Rowlett, Scott & Associates

St. Anselm's Priory for the Benedictine Fathers, Tokyo, Japan; Antonin Raymond & L. L. Rado

Chapel of the Holy Cross, Sedona, Ariz.; Anshen and Allen

AWARDS OF MERIT

Residence, Mason B. Wells, Belvedere, Calif.; Edward B. Page

Wyeth Laboratories, Inc., Radnor, Pa.; Skidmore, Owings & Merrill

Memorial Hall for Japanese Steel Workers, Kyushu, Japan; Antonin Raymond & L. L. Rado

Tokeneke Elementary School, Darien, Conn.; R. B. O'Connor; W. H. Kilham, Jr.; Philip M. Chu

The Medical Towers, Houston, Tex.; Golemon & Rolfe

Residence-Studio, Raleigh, N. C.; George Matsumoto

Mark Thomas Inn Additions, Del Monte, Monterey, Calif.; John Carl Warnecke

Residence, Mr. and Mrs. A. Quincy Jones, Los Angeles, Calif.; A. Quincy Jones; Frederick E. Emmons

Our Lady of the Sea General Hospital, Golden Meadow, La.; Curtis & Davis

Residence, Mr. and Mrs. Frederick E. Emmons, Pacific Palisades, Calif.; A. Quincy Jones; Frederick E. Emmons

Rich's Department Store, Knoxville, Tenn.; Stevens & Wilkinson

Wilson Junior High School, Charlotte, N. C.; Arthur Gould Odell, Jr.

San Jacinto Elementary School, Liberty, Tex.; Caudill, Rowlett, Scott and Associates

Northeast Branch Public Library, Seattle, Wash.; Paul Thiry

1958

FIRST HONOR AWARDS

Home Office Building, Bloomfield, Conn.; Skidmore, Owings & Merrill

Pharmaceutical Plant Headquarters, Pasadena, Calif.; Edward D. Stone

Elementary School, Sonoma County, Calif.; Mario J. Ciampi

Westmoor High School, Daly City, Calif.; Mario J. Ciampi

Robinson's Specialty Shop, Palm Springs, Calif.; Pereira & Luckman

AWARDS OF MERIT

Warm Mineral Springs Inn, Venice, Fla.; Victor A. Lundy

Studio, Pasadena, Calif.; Thornton Ladd

Cafeteria Building, Southeastern Louisiana College, Hammond, La.; Desmond & Davis

Residence, Mr. and Mrs. Neil Lakenan, Beverly Hills, Calif.; Richard Dorman & Associates

Union Service Center, Los Angeles, Calif.; Smith & Williams

Washington State Bank, Bellevue Office, Bellevue, Wash.; Mithun & Nesland

Immaculate Conception Church, Marrero, La.; Curtis and Davis; Harrison Schouest

U. S. Pavilion, Universal and International Exposition, Brussels, Belgium; Edward D. Stone

Beckman/Helipot Corporation Plant, Newport Beach, Calif.; Pereira & Luckman

1959

FIRST HONOR AWARDS

Diaz-Simon Pediatric Clinic, New Orleans, La.; Charles R. Colbert

Central Service Facility, Spokane, Wash.; Kenneth W. Brooks; Bruce M. Walker

McGregor Memorial Community Conference Center, Detroit, Mich.; Minoru Yamasaki & Associates

Concordia Senior College, Fort Wayne, Ind.; Eero Saarinen & Associates

Zeckendorf Plaza Development, May-D & F Dept. Store, Denver, Colo.; I. M. Pei & Associates

AWARDS OF MERIT

Florida's Silver Springs (Tourist Center), Silver Springs, Fla.; Victor A. Lundy
Temple Emanu-El, Dallas, Tex.; Howard R. Meyer; Max M. Sandfield; William W. Wurster
Benjamin Franklin Junior High School, Wayne, Mich.; Minoru Yamasaki & Associates
San Angelo Central High School, San Angelo, Tex.; Caudill, Rowlett & Scott; Max D. Lovett
Residence, Mr. and Mrs. Dunbar Carpenter, Medford, Ore.; George T. Rockrise
Tradewell Market, Burien, King County, Wash.; Welton D. Becket and Associates; Rushmore & Woodman
Residence, Mr. and Mrs. Richard Beattie, Rye, N. Y.; Ulrich Franzen
Mile High Center, Denver, Colo.; I. M. Pei & Associates; Kahn & Jacobs
Residence, Mr. and Mrs. John Black Lee, New Canaan, Conn.; John Black Lee
Gretna Methodist Church, Gretna, La.; Lawrence & Saunders

1960

FIRST HONOR AWARDS

Mutual Insurance Company of Hartford, Hartford, Conn.; Sherwood, Mills and Smith;
Moore School of Electrical Engineering, Philadelphia, Pa.; Robert L. Geddes; Melvin Brecher; Warren W. Cunningham
Residence, Mr. and Mrs. Richard Opdahl, Long Beach, Calif.; Killingsworth, Brady and Smith
Blyth Arena, Squaw Valley, Calif.; Corlett and Spackman; Kitchen and Hunt
U. S. Embassy Office Building, Oslo, Norway; Eero Saarinen & Associates

AWARDS OF MERIT

International Minerals & Chemical Corporation, Skokie, Ill.; Perkins & Will
St. Paul's Lutheran Church (Fellowship Hall), Sarasota, Fla.; Victor A. Lundy
Lenox Square Shopping Center, Atlanta, Ga.; Toombs, Amisano & Wells
Builder's House, Mill Valley, Calif.; Raphael S. Soriano
Residence, Alyn B. Reid, Mill Valley, Calif.; Lee Stuart Darrow
Clemens Homes, Mount Clemens, Mich.; Meathe, Kessler & Associates, Inc.
National Airlines Nose Hangar, Miami, Fla.; Weed, Johnson Associates
Industrial Reactor Laboratories, Plainsborough, N. J.; Skidmore, Owings & Merrill
Asilomar Housing, Pacific Grove, Calif.; John Carl Warnecke & Associates
The Capitol Park Apartments, Washington, D. C.; Satterlee & Smith
The Church of the Redeemer, Baltimore, Md.; Pietro Belluschi; Rogers, Taliaferro & Lamb

1961

FIRST HONOR AWARDS

U. S. Embassy, New Delhi, India; Edward D. Stone
Fernando Rivera Elementary School, Daly City, Calif.; Mario J. Ciampi; Paul Reiter
Roofless Church, New Harmony, Ind.; Philip Johnson
Reynolds Metals Regional Sales Office Building, Detroit, Mich.; Minoru Yamasaki
Nuclear Reactor, Rehovot, Israel; Philip Johnson
Pepsi-Cola World Headquarters, New York, N. Y.; Skidmore, Owings & Merrill
Summer House, Mr. and Mrs. Alan Schwartz, Northville, Mich.; Birkerts and Straub

AWARDS OF MERIT

Ivory Tower Restaurant, Santa Monica, Calif.; Richard Dorman & Associates
Denver Hilton Hotel, Denver, Colo.; I. M. Pei & Associates
Marin Bay Display Pavilion, San Rafael, Calif.; Bay Group Associates
Office & Warehouse for The Coppertone Corp., Miami, Fla.; Weed-Johnson-Associates
Residence, Dr. Henry G. Simon, New Orleans, La.; Charles R. Colbert
Chapel, Moline Public Hospital, Moline, Ill.; Henry Hill; John W. Kruse
Office Building for a Development Firm, Long Beach, Calif.; Killingsworth, Brady, Smith and Associates
The Unitarian Church, Concord, N. H.; Hugh Stubbins and Associates
Crown Zellerbach Building, San Francisco, Calif.; Hertzka & Knowles; Skidmore, Owings & Merrill
Lincoln Commons Building, Lake Erie College, Painesville, Ohio; Victor Christ-Janer and Associates
Willow Creek Apartments, Palo Alto, Calif.; John Carl Warnecke and Associates

BIOGRAPHICAL NOTES

THORNTON ABELL, Los Angeles, Calif. Abell received his education at the universities of Michigan and Southern California. He has been in private practice since 1944, with work consisting of residential, school and commercial buildings.

ROBERT E. ALEXANDER, FAIA, Los Angeles, Calif. Alexander studied at Cornell University. After being with various firms in New York and Los Angeles, he formed a partnership firm with Richard Neutra from 1948 to 1958. He has recently returned to an independent practice. He has been a member of the faculty of the University of Southern California since 1952 and was visiting critic at Cornell in 1952–53.

ALLISON & RIBLE, Los Angeles, Calif. George B. Allison, FAIA, and Ulysses Floyd Rible, FAIA, formed their partnership in 1944. Rodney T. Robinson and Raymond Ziegler were admitted in 1958. They have a widely diversified practice, principally industrial, educational, and institutional projects.

ANDERSON, BECKWITH AND HAIBLE, Boston, Mass. The firm was started in 1938 by Professors Lawrence B. Anderson and Herbert L. Beckwith, FAIA. Many major MIT buildings were built during and following World War II, including the Swimming Pool and the Biology Laboratory. Foreign work includes the Philippine American Life Insurance Company in Manila and the U. S. Embassy at Taipei.

ANSHEN AND ALLEN, San Francisco, Calif. The firm was founded in 1940 by S. Robert Anshen and William Stephen Allen, FAIA. Both are graduates of the University of Pennsylvania. The firm has received a number of awards for excellence in design. In addition, it has done architectural and interior design of passenger accommodations for several freighters and ocean liners.

WARREN H. ASHLEY, West Hartford, Conn. Ashley studied at Syracuse University. The present firm was opened in 1952. He has a general architectural practice, including among his principal works numerous schools in Connecticut, Massachusetts, and New York.

ASSOCIATED ARCHITECTS AND ENGINEERS, Pasadena, Calif. Members of the firm were Whitney R. Smith, FAIA, A. Quincy Jones, FAIA, and Edgardo Contini. The firm has been dissolved; Smith is now a partner in the firm working under the name of Smith and Williams, Architects and Engineers; Jones is now a partner of the firm of Jones and Emmons; and Contini of Victor Gruen and Associates. Each of these firms is performing architectural and planning services on a national and international scale in all types of construction.

Donald Barthelme, faia, Houston, Tex. Barthelme is a graduate of the University of Pennsylvania. He was professor of architectural design at the University of Houston and Rice Institute, and received the São Paulo Biennial prize in 1952. He formed his own firm in 1939.

Bassetti & Morse, Seattle, Wash. Fred Bassetti studied at the universities of Washington and Harvard; John M. Morse at Harvard. They established their firm in 1947, and are responsible for such structures as college buildings at the University of Washington, Western Washington State College, and Central Washington State College; medical clinics, schools, a prison, housing projects, airport buildings, and many private residences. They also maintain an office in Hawaii.

Bay Group Associates, San Francisco, Calif. This group of architects including Daniel H. Bushnell, Lun Chan, Ichiro Sasaki, and Camiel Van De Weghe, came together through agreement on a basic form of practice and with consideration for their varying interests and specializations within the field of architecture. They are all products of California schools and colleges. Their collective name is indicative of the principal area of their practice.

Welton Becket, faia, Los Angeles, Calif. Becket, president of Welton Becket and Associates, is a graduate of the University of Washington and studied at Le École des Beaux-Arts in Fontainebleau. His multitude of projects includes the Prudential Insurance building in Los Angeles, the Beverly Hilton Hotel in Beverly Hills, Kaiser Center in Oakland, and Southland Center in Dallas.

William S. Beckett, Los Angeles, Calif. Beckett studied at Yale and he was later chief designer for Sumner Spaulding, and served on the faculty of the University of California. He opened his own architectural office in 1949. His work was included in the 1953 Biennial Exhibition, São Paulo, and the Gold Medal Exhibit of the Architectural League of New York.

Pietro Belluschi, faia, Cambridge, Mass. A native of Italy, Belluschi studied at the University of Rome, coming to the U. S. in 1923 through one of the first exchange scholarships between Italy and America. Here he studied at Cornell. After a number of years as a member and then head of an architectural firm in the Northwest, he left the firm to assume duties as dean of the School of Architecture and Planning at MIT.

Birkerts & Straub, Birmingham, Mich. Gunnar Birkerts studied at the Technische Hochschule, Stuttgart, and Frank Straub at the University of Michigan. Both were formerly associated with Minoru Yamasaki before opening their own office in 1960. They have received a number of international and national awards for architectural design.

Kenneth W. Brooks and Bruce M. Walker, Spokane, Wash. Brooks received his education at the University of Illinois and established his Spokane office of Kenneth W. Brooks & Associates in 1950 after being on the design staff of Skidmore, Owings & Merrill. Walker studied at the University of Washington and Harvard Graduate School of Design. They joined their small individual offices to design the Washington Water Power project.

Arthur T. Brown, faia, Tucson, Ariz. Brown received his education at Tarkio College, Missouri, and Ohio State. He formed his firm in 1942 and has a general architectural practice. His work consists of residences, churches, schools, and commercial buildings.

William Hoskins Brown, Boston, Mass. Brown studied at MIT. He formed his present firm in 1938 and has such structures as apartments, powerhouses, bridges, and college buildings to his credit.

Caudill, Rowlett, Scott and Associates, Houston, Tex. The firm was founded in 1946 when William W. Caudill and John M. Rowlett opened an office in Austin, Texas. Today the firm maintains its home office in Houston and includes engineers and city planners as well as architects. Regional offices are located in Oklahoma City and Stamford, Connecticut. The firm has won numerous national awards for excellence in design.

Chaix and Johnson, Los Angeles, Calif. Principals in the firm are Alfred V. Chaix and

Ralph W. Johnson. Some of the significant buildings designed by the firm are St. Albert's Catholic Church; Lutheran Church of Our Redeemer; St. Paul the Apostle Catholic Church; St. Brigid Catholic Church; St. Hilary Convent and Nativity Catholic Church.

VICTOR CHRIST-JANER AND ASSOCIATES, New Canaan, Conn. Christ-Janer received his training at St. Olaf College and Yale University. He established his own firm in 1955 and has completed such projects as the U. S. Consulate General Office Building, Rotterdam, and the United Church, West Norwalk, Connecticut. He has taught at Stephens College, Columbia, Missouri, and has been visiting critic at Yale and Columbia universities.

MARIO J. CIAMPI, FAIA, San Francisco, Calif. Ciampi studied at Harvard University Graduate School of Architecture and Beaux-Arts Institute of Design, Paris. He has devoted much time to promotion of art in architecture in public buildings and has been lecturer at the schools of architecture, University of California, Stanford University, San Francisco State, and University of Southern California.

CLARK AND BEUTTLER, San Francisco, Calif. Hervey P. Clark, FAIA, and William L. Beuttler formed their firm in 1946. Their varied architectural practice includes such structures as residences, churches, commercial, and industrial buildings.

ALEXANDER S. COCHRAN, Baltimore, Md. Cochran is a graduate of Harvard and was visiting lecturer there 1951-58. He is a member of the firm of Cochran, Stephenson & Wing. Some of the projects executed by this firm are: U. S. Consulate, Nagoya, Japan; Church of Our Saviour; Baltimore City Hospitals Addition; Suburban Club; Sheraton-Baltimore Inn; Lion Brothers Office & Plant—all in Baltimore.

COCKE, BOWMAN AND YORK, Harlingen, Tex. Bartlett Cocke, FAIA, and John G. York, studied at the University of Texas; Walter C. Bowman at Louisiana Polytechnic Institute. They formed their partnership firm in 1949. Since 1954 they have severally had independent firms.

COLBERT AND LOWREY, New Orleans, La. Charles R. Colbert is a principal in the firm of Colbert, Lowrey, Hess and Boudreaux, which was formed in 1960. From 1957–1959 he was a principal, with Mark Perrin Lowrey, in the firm of Colbert and Lowrey and Associates. He studied at the Universities of Texas, Michigan, Columbia and Loyola and is currently dean of the School of Architecture, Columbia University.

EDGARDO CONTINI, *see* ASSOCIATED ARCHITECTS AND ENGINEERS

MARIO FRANCIS CORBETT, San Francisco, Calif. Corbett studied at the San Francisco School of Fine Arts. He lectured in architecture at the University of California and was visiting critic in architecture at Yale University. He has practiced architecture in the Bay region since 1933, when he formed his own firm in San Francisco. Major buildings designed consist of residences, commercial structures, schools, and churches.

CORLETT AND SPACKMAN, KITCHEN AND HUNT, San Francisco, Calif. William Corlett and Wendell Spackman are both graduates of the University of California. They formed the firm of Corlett and Spackman in 1954. Robert S. Kitchen, a graduate of Cornell, and Frank B. Hunt, a graduate of the universities of Nebraska and California, formed their firm in 1948. All facilities for the 1960 Olympic Winter Games in Squaw Valley were designed by a joint venture of the two firms.

CURTIS & DAVIS, New Orleans, La. Nathaniel C. Curtis, Jr., studied at Tulane, and Arthur Quentin Davis, FAIA, studied at Tulane and Harvard. Their partnership was formed in 1946, and since then this firm has won top awards for its work both in New Orleans and such far-flung places as San Juan, Puerto Rico, and Berlin.

GEORGE LEIGHTON DAHL, FAIA, Dallas, Tex. Dahl studied at the University of Minnesota and Harvard, with postgraduate work at American Academy in Rome. He worked as designer for Myron Hunt and H. C. Chambers in Los Angeles and Herbert M. Greene in Dallas before he opened his own firm in 1928. In addition to his architectural practice, which covers such building types as offices, warehouses, housing projects, department stores, banks and institutions, he has been a leader in public service and currently serves as a member of the Dallas City Plan Advisory Committee.

DANIEL, MANN, JOHNSON & MENDENHALL, Los Angeles, Calif. The firm was originally comprised of Philip J. Daniel, Arthur E. Mann, and S. Kenneth Johnson, with Irvan F. Mendenhall joining the partnership later. The firm has designed numerous office buildings; defense, missile, engineering, and heavy construction projects; a $20-million urban renewal complex; apartment houses, schools, and commercial buildings.

LEE STUART DARROW, Oakland, Calif. Darrow studied at the University of California, under Eric Mendelsohn. Before opening his own office in 1959, he gained experience by working with several well-known architects—John Lyon Reid, FAIA, Mario Corbett, and John Carl Warnecke. His Alyn Reid residence won five different awards and honors.

WILLIAM HENLEY DEITRICK, FAIA, Raleigh, N. C. Deitrick studied at Wake Forest College and Columbia University. He established his present firm of William H. Deitrick & Associates in Raleigh. He has been President of the North Carolina State College Design Foundation since 1959 and was co-winner of the Gold Medal in Engineering, New York Architectural League, in 1953.

VERNON DE MARS, Berkeley, Calif. De Mars studied at the University of California, where he is now teaching. In addition, he maintains an office in Berkeley. Some of the principal works of his architectural firm include apartments, residences, and rural and public housing.

DESMOND & DAVIS, Hammond, La. John J. Desmond studied at Tulane University and MIT. A. Jackson Davis studied at Alabama Polytechnic Institute. Their partnership firm was founded in 1956 and its work was comprised mostly of schools and commercial buildings. Since 1959 Desmond has been partner in the firm of Desmond-Miremont & Associates.

RICHARD DORMAN & ASSOCIATES, Beverly Hills, Calif. Richard Dorman & Associates was founded in 1956 and has produced residential, office building, hotel, motel, and restaurant design. Significant buildings are: the Lakenan and Landis residences: vault-roof house in Sherman Oaks (a New York Architectural League award winner); and the Briggs Skytop residence.

ALDEN B. DOW, FAIA, Midland, Mich. After studying mechanical engineering for three years at the University of Michigan, Dow changed his course and enrolled in the School of Architecture at Columbia. In the fall of 1933, he spent five months with Frank Lloyd Wright; afterward he opened his own office for general practice in Midland. Listed among his awards are the "Diplome de Grand Prix," given by the Paris International Exposition for residential architecture in the United States; and the 1960 Gold Medal of the Michigan Society of Architects.

G. A. DOWNS, Carmel, Calif. Downs studied at Pennsylvania State University, Princeton, and MIT. He was awarded the thirty-second Paris Prize in Architecture in 1939. After a number of years in federal employ, he began his own firm in 1948.

JAMES D. FESSENDEN, San Francisco, Calif. Fessenden studied at Rensselaer and Alabama polytechnic institutes. Since 1953 he has been a member of the firm, Ernest J. Kump & Associates, with his principal work consisting mainly of schools.

ULRICH FRANZEN, New York, N. Y. Franzen was educated at Williams College and Harvard University. He has been on the architectural faculties of Yale, Carnegie Institute of Technology, Washington University in St. Louis, and Harvard. Besides being on various architectural committees, Franzen is also active in the furtherance of his profession as chairman of the Architectural Board of Review, Rye, New York.

KENNETH FRANZHEIM, FAIA, Houston, Tex. Franzheim was a graduate of MIT and practiced architecture in New York for a number of years before opening his office in Houston. He was associate architect on the Fairlington Housing Project in Washington, and supervising architect, Reconstruction Finance Corporation, Washington. Mr. Franzheim died in 1959.

FRERET AND WOLF, New Orleans, La. The firm of Freret and Wolf was founded in 1946 by Douglass V. Freret and Albert J. Wolf, Jr. Freret studied at Tulane and Cornell universities; Wolf at Yale. The firm's practice is devoted largely to institutional and ecclesiastical work throughout the South.

GEDDES, BRECHER, QUALLS, AND CUNNINGHAM, Philadelphia, Pa. The office was established in 1953, with other partners joining in 1957 and 1960. The firm is small, averaging ten persons. In addition to their practice, Geddes and Qualls teach at the University of Pennsylvania. Robert L. Geddes and Melvin Brecher are graduates of Harvard; George W. Qualls of the University of Oklahoma and North Carolina State College; and Warren W. Cunningham of Franklin and Marshall College and the University of Pennsylvania. The Moore School of Electrical Engineering for which they won a 1960 AIA Honor Award was the firm's first building.

GIFFELS AND VALLET, INC., Detroit, Mich. Louis Rossetti, FAIA, joined the firm of Giffels and Vallet, Inc., as an architect in 1928; the partnership later became Giffels and Rossetti, and provides a complete architectural-engineering service for the design and engineering of industrial and institutional structures.

GOLEMON & ROLFE, Houston and Beaumont, Tex. Albert S. Golemon, FAIA, studied at Alabama Polytechnic Institute, MIT, and Fontainebleau; Walter T. Rolfe, FAIA, at Kansas State College and MIT. They formed their partnership in 1946 and have had a broad general practice.

CHARLES M. GOODMAN, FAIA, Washington, D.C. Goodman has been called the "Production House Architect." He operates his own firm and is architect for the nation's largest prefabricator of housing, and for leading builders in the Washington area.

MICHAEL GOODMAN, Berkeley, Calif. Goodman graduated from the University of California, where he is now professor of architecture. He also has his own firm which he established in 1934, projects of which include San Mateo County Hall of Justice and Records and office buildings for East Bay Municipal Utility District.

VICTOR GRUEN, FAIA, New York, N. Y. Gruen is senior partner in Victor Gruen Associates, Los Angeles, New York, and Chicago. He pioneered in regional shopping centers: Eastland, Detroit; Southdale, Minneapolis, and others. He is equally known for urban renewal, redevelopment projects: Midtown Plaza, Rochester, New York; Fresno, California; Paterson, New Jersey; Stamford, Connecticut, and others. He was creator of the widely adapted "Fort Worth Plan."

HARRISON, ABRAMOVITZ & ABBE, New York, N. Y. When the award-winning Corning Glass Center was built, the firm was pioneering in the use of various materials for building curtain walls. The United Nations Secretariat, for which Wallace K. Harrison, FAIA, was director of planning, and Max Abramovitz, FAIA, deputy director, was the first use of a full glass wall for a skyscraper. Later, the firm designed the Corning Glass Works Building in New York which employs more glass than any other building ever built. The present firm is principally known for its large office buildings, and has designed many buildings for college campuses.

WILLIAM B. HARVARD, St. Petersburg, Fla. Harvard is a native of Florida, attended the University of Cincinnati and worked in Miami prior to opening his office in St. Petersburg. After serving five years in the army, he resumed practice in St. Petersburg with John B. Dodd as associate; later Blanchard Jolly, who is now a partner, joined him.

HELLMUTH, YAMASAKI & LEINWEBER, Detroit, Mich. and St. Louis, Mo. The firm of Hellmuth, Yamasaki & Leinweber was organized in 1949. Principal members of the firm were Joseph W. Leinweber, Minoru Yamasaki, FAIA, and George F. Hellmuth. Hellmuth is now associated with Obata & Kassabaum in St. Louis, Leinweber is presently engaged in the Far East, while Yamasaki has his own firm in Birmingham, Michigan.

HERTZKA & KNOWLES, San Francisco, Calif. Hertzka and Knowles was founded in 1933 by Wayne S. Hertzka, FAIA, and William H. Knowles. Robert P. Tobin and George S. Dolim are associates. The firm's projects of note include Headquarters Office Building, Pacific Telephone Company, Sacramento, and office buildings for the America Fore Loyalty Group and the State Bar of California.

HENRY HILL, San Francisco, Calif. Hill received his education at the universities of California and Harvard. He began work in the office of John E. Dinwiddie, which later became the partnership of Dinwiddie & Hill; Eric Mendelsohn joined the firm in 1946. In 1957 he established his present office with John W. Kruse as associate. Hill has served as visiting lecturer at Stanford, Cornell, University of California, and at Kansas, Utah and Oregon.

David H. Horn, M. D. Mortland, Fresno, Calif. Horn, principal member of the firm, is a graduate of the University of California, and opened his office to practice in Fresno in 1935. Buildings designed include residences; tract and public housing; commercial, industrial, religious, and public buildings; schools and hospitals. Present name of firm is David H. Horn, Marshall D. Mortland, Richard P. Clark, Associate Architects.

James M. Hunter, faia, Boulder, Colo. In 1940 Hunter and Harold Stuart Jones formed a partnership which was dissolved on the death of Mr. Jones in 1945. Hunter is senior partner and principal of the present firm. In 1958 he was invited, along with nine other urban planners and architects, by the West German government to discuss with German architects and planners Germany's post-war planning and reconstruction programs. He is currently the National Second Vice-President, AIA.

Delp W. Johnson, San Francisco, Calif. Johnson studied at the University of California, served as draftsman in the firm of Thomsen & Wilson, and since 1955 as associate of firm of Ernest J. Kump & Associates. His principal work has been in the design of schools.

Philip Johnson, New York, N. Y. Johnson is a graduate of Harvard. Before opening his firm in New York in 1953, he was director of architecture at the Museum of Modern Art, New York City. His "Glass House" and "Wiley House" in New Canaan, Connecticut, have enhanced his reputation as an architect.

A. Quincy Jones, Jr., Frederick E. Emmons, Los Angeles, Calif. Jones, FAIA, studied at the University of Washington; Emmons at Cornell. They formed their partnership firm in 1950, and have designed such varied projects as factories, residences, swimming pools, and community centers.

Kahn & Jacobs, New York, N. Y. Products of Columbia University Architecture School, Jacques Ely Kahn and Robert Allen Jacobs are fellows of the American Institute of Architects. They formed their partnership in 1941.

George Fred Keck, William Keck, Chicago, Ill. George Fred Keck received his education at the University of Illinois. He began his own practice in 1927. Immediately following graduation from the same university, William Keck joined the office; he became a partner in 1946. The firm specializes in housing.

Kelly & Gruzen, New York, N. Y. B. Sumner Gruzen, FAIA, principal of Kelly & Gruzen, received his education at MIT and did graduate work in Europe as holder of the Rotch Architectural Scholarship. His practice has encompassed work in diversified fields, including large-scale housing and urban renewal, schools and universities, public works and hospitals.

Robert Woods Kennedy, Cambridge, Mass. Kennedy studied at both the Beaux-Arts in Paris and Harvard, and at one time worked for Walter Gropius, FAIA, and Marcel Breuer, FAIA. From the end of the war until 1952 he taught architectural design at MIT. He now has his own practice.

Ketchum, Gina & Sharp, New York, N. Y. Morris Ketchum, Jr., FAIA, and J. Stanley Sharp are partners in the firm of Ketchum and Sharp, which succeeded Ketchum, Gina & Sharp. Ketchum has designed stores, shopping centers, and shops in thirty of the fifty states as well as in South America and Europe. He has also planned schools, office buildings, and factories. Sharp is widely known for his school planning.

Keyes, Smith, Satterlee & Lethbridge, Washington, D. C. Arthur H. Keyes studied at Deerfield Academy, Princeton and Harvard universities; Chloethiel Woodard Smith, FAIA, at the University of Oregon and Washington University; Nicholas Satterlee at Hotchkiss School and Harvard; Francis D. Lethbridge at Stevens Institute of Technology, University of Colorado and Yale University. Their firm, organized in 1951, is now dissolved. Two new firms have succeeded; the one, Satterlee and Smith and Keyes; the other, Lethbridge and Condon.

Killingsworth, Brady and Smith, Long Beach, Calif. The firm is a partnership of Edward A. Killingsworth, Jules Brady and

Waugh Smith. Killingsworth and Brady are graduates of the University of Southern California, Smith of University of California. The work of the firm has spread from small residential projects to multi-million dollar institutional architecture.

KITCHEN AND HUNT, *see* CORLETT AND SPACKMAN

VINCENT G. KLING, FAIA, Philadelphia, Pa. Kling studied at Columbia and MIT. He established his architectural firm in 1946 and has received numerous national, state, and local awards and honors for architectural design. As consultant to the Philadelphia City Planning Commission, he helped to develop the original master plan for the Penn Center Development in Philadelphia and later designed the Transportation Center Building and much of the five-block Penn Center Concourse.

CARL KOCH, FAIA, Cambridge, Mass. Koch studied at Harvard, gaining working experience in the office of Gropius and Breuer before starting his own firm in 1946. He has served as assistant professor of architecture at MIT and as visiting critic, Yale University School of Architecture.

ERNEST J. KUMP & ASSOCIATES, Palo Alto, Calif. Kump studied at the University of California and Harvard. He established the present firm in 1950. Kump, with various associates, has, over a number of years, developed an architecture based on a firmly-held philosophy of order and principle in design, adapted to the technology of this century, yet respectful of regional and functional expression and of human values.

THORNTON LADD, Pasadena, Calif. Ladd studied at the University of Southern California, working for a general contractor and then in the offices of two architects. He now has his own practice with offices in Santa Barbara and Pasadena.

FREDERICK L. LANGHORST, Berkeley, Calif. Langhorst studied at Cornell and with Frank Lloyd Wright at Taliesin. His experience includes work with William W. Wurster and Daniel, Mann, Johnson & Mendenhall and several overseas assignments. He has received numerous awards for his buildings; he lectures on architecture and has served on several planning groups.

LAWRENCE AND SAUNDERS, Metaire, La. John W. Lawrence studied at Tulane and Columbia universities and is at present dean in the School of Architecture, Tulane. George A. Saunders studied at Oklahoma University, North Carolina State and MIT. Their firm has received numerous honors and awards for various buildings.

JOHN BLACK LEE, New Canaan, Conn. Lee received his B.A. from Brown University. He learned architecture in the offices of Paul Schweikher, FAIA, Oskar Stonorov, FAIA, and Eliot Noyes, FAIA. He has had his own practice since 1954. His work has been exhibited by the New York Architectural League, New Haven Festival of Arts, and American Federation of Arts. He has also served on juries and as visiting critic at Yale University.

ROGER LEE, Berkeley, Calif. Lee studied at the University of California and organized his own firm in 1948 after a previous association with Fred Langhorst.

ROBERT M. LITTLE, WILLIAM G. CRAWFORD, Miami and Fort Lauderdale, Fla. Little, a Regional Director of AIA, was educated at the University of California. He opened his own firm in Miami, some of the principal work of which is the Merrick Building and Ring Theatre of the University of Miami. Crawford studied at the University of Florida and was in partnership with Little from 1946 to 1953. He now has his own firm.

FRANCIS E. LLOYD, San Francisco, Calif. Lloyd studied at the University of Pennsylvania. Before starting practice he studied in Europe and worked in major offices in New York and San Francisco. His work has consisted of residences, housing projects, commercial and institutional buildings, as well as naval installations.

LUNDGREN & MAURER, Austin, Tex. Both Leonard J. Lundgren and Edward Maurer studied at the University of Texas and received their architectural training in several Texas architects' offices. They formed their partnership in 1953 and subsequently have won awards for their designs.

VICTOR A. LUNDY, Sarasota, Fla. and New York, N. Y. Lundy was educated at Harvard and the University of Maine. In 1957–58 he served on the architectural faculties of Harvard and the University of Florida. The major portion of his diversified architectural practice since the establishment of his firm in 1954 has been in the state of Florida.

MAYNARD LYNDON, FAIA, Los Angeles, Calif. Lyndon studied at the University of Michigan and practiced in Detroit for six years with Eberle M. Smith as Lyndon and Smith. He began private practice in Los Angeles in 1942 in general architecture.

FRANCIS JOSEPH MCCARTHY, FAIA, San Francisco, Calif. McCarthy was educated at Stanford University and has had his own practice since 1938. In addition, he has filled such positions as art commissioner in San Francisco, 1949–51, and has been on the faculty of Stanford University from 1955 to the present time. Significant buildings of his design include the Southern Inyo Hospital, Inyo County Library, and Electrical Union Office Building and Auditorium.

MCFARLAND, BONSALL & THOMAS, Los Angeles, Calif. Philip D. McFarland studied at the universities of Washington and Southern California and at the École des Beaux-Arts, Paris; Wallace C. Bonsall at the University of Minnesota and Harvard. The present firm of McFarland & Bonsall was formed in 1954; its principal works consist of schools, residences and commercial structures.

MARRACCINI AND PATTERSON, *see* STONE AND MULLOY

MARSH, SMITH AND POWELL, Los Angeles, Calif. Smith, Powell and Morgridge and its predecessor firm, Marsh, Smith and Powell, have designed educational plants and civic buildings since 1927. The firm's members are D. D. Smith, Herbert Powell, FAIA, Howard Morgridge, Albert Richards and Redmond Coghlan.

MILTON FOY MARTIN, Houston, Tex. Martin studied at Texas A. and M. College. He was in private practice until 1955 when he formed a partnership with George W. Rustay. As an individual practitioner, he designed the Texas Children's Hospital. As partner in firm of Rustay & Martin, he designed Calhoun County Court House, Port Lavaca, Texas, and First Church of Christ, Scientist, Houston.

MARTIN, STEWART & NOBLE, Philadelphia, Pa. This firm was established in 1954, the principals being Sydney E. Martin, FAIA, Harry G. Stewart, and Robert W. Noble. The major projects designed by the firm, or the partners as individuals, include important institutional work in the Philadelphia region.

CARL L. MASTON, Los Angeles, Calif. Maston studied at the University of Southern California to which he returned in 1953 as visiting design critic. He has had a continual practice since 1941 except for three years' service in the Marine Corps. He has won a number of national awards.

GEORGE MATSUMOTO, Raleigh, N. C. Matsumoto studied at the University of California, Washington University, and Cranbrook Academy of Art. He has a private practice in Missouri, North Carolina, and Virginia, and has won many national competitions and awards. In 1947–48 he taught at the University of Oklahoma, and 1948–61 at the North Carolina State College.

MEATHE, KESSLER AND ASSOCIATES, Grosse Pointe, Mich. The Office of Meathe, Kessler and Associates was formed in 1955 and has been engaged in the design of all types of buildings. The principals of the firm are Philip J. Meathe, William Kessler and Eugene Dilaura. In addition to several local awards, the firm has received three awards in the AIA Homes for Better Living competition.

HOWARD R. MEYER, FAIA, Dallas, Tex. Meyer received his education at Columbia University. His training included working in several large architectural offices in New York and with the well-known church architects, The Bertram C. Goodhue Associates. In 1935 he moved his practice to Dallas and has been increasingly active in professional and civic affairs.

MITHUN & NESLAND, Seattle, Wash. The firm of Mithun & Nesland has been dissolved. Omer L. Mithun is now a partner in the firm of Mithun, Ridenour & Cochran and Harold J. Nesland has his own firm in Seattle.

W. C. Muchow, Denver, Colo. Muchow studied at the University of Illinois and Cranbrook Academy. He won the Rome prize in architecture in 1948; in 1951 he was awarded the Plym Fellowship of the University of Illinois for travel in Europe. He has served on the architectural faculties at the University of Illinois and the University of Colorado. Several of his outstanding buildings are: First Federal Savings & Loan Association, Muchow residence, Merino Elementary School, and Brentwood Methodist Church.

Wallace Neff, FAIA, Los Angeles, Calif. Neff has his architectural practice in Los Angeles and has designed such well-known buildings as "Pickfair," the residence of Douglas Fairbanks and Mary Pickford; three buildings for Loyola University; Doheny Memorial Dormitory in Washington, D. C.; and Doheny Memorial Library, Camarillo, California. He is also the inventor of pneumatic forming.

Richard J. Neutra, FAIA, Dion Neutra, Los Angeles, Calif. Austrian-born Neutra has lived and worked in America since 1923. He holds national and foreign registrations, and has received innumerable national and international architectural awards for various projects. He has a widely diversified practice. Dion Neutra received his education at the Swiss Federal Institute of Technology, Zurich, and the University of California. He has been an associate in his father's firm since 1955.

Eliot Noyes, FAIA, New Canaan, Conn. Noyes received his education at Harvard College and Harvard Graduate School of Design. He established his firm in 1947. Previous to that he had worked for Gropius and Breuer. He also served for three years as Associate Professor of Architectural Design at Yale and is a member of the Town Planning Advisory Commission, New Canaan. His best-known buildings are the Bubble Houses in Florida, the Noyes residence in New Canaan, and the IBM Education Center in Poughkeepsie.

O'Connor and Kilham, New York, N. Y. R. B. O'Connor, FAIA, and W. H. Kilham, Jr., FAIA, organized their firm in 1943, continuing the architectural practice of Morris and O'Connor, and of Van der Gracht and Kilham. Their recent work has included the Firestone Library, Princeton University; the Phoenix Insurance Building, Hartford, Connecticut, and the new National Library of Medicine in Washington.

A. G. Odell, Jr., FAIA, Charlotte, N. C. Odell studied at Duke and Cornell universities, and spent a year at the École des Beaux-Arts in Paris. In 1940 he organized his present firm in Charlotte and has had a continuous practice there except when with the Corps of Engineers during World War II. The honors awarded his firm are many. Included among notable structures are: Wilson Junior High, which won four separate awards, and the Charlotte Auditorium and Coliseum.

O'Dell, Hewlett and Luckenbach, Birmingham, Mich. H. Augustus O'Dell began architectural practice in 1903 in Detroit with the firm of Baxter and O'Dell; Thomas H. Hewlett in Cleveland in 1923; and Owen A. Luckenbach in Detroit in 1932. Hewlett and Luckenbach formed a partnership firm in 1936. O'Dell joined them in 1942, forming the present firm, which has a widely diversified practice.

Pace Associates, Chicago, Ill. Organized as a firm of planners, architects, and consulting engineers in 1946, Pace Associates has designed several mining towns as well as a number of apartments, and educational, commercial, and industrial buildings. The firm was responsible for the engineering, construction supervision, and budget determination of several of Mies van der Rohe's prominent buildings. Partners include Charles B. Genther, W. H. Binford, and John F. Kausal.

Edward B. Page, San Francisco, Calif. Page studied at Yale University and has had his own practice in San Francisco since 1947. Among buildings which he has designed are the Home Office of Fireman's Fund Insurance Company in San Francisco and branch offices for that company in Los Angeles, San Jose, and Atlanta.

I. M. Pei & Associates, New York, N. Y. The firm has a staff of seventy-five people including city planners, graphic artists, and architectural modelmakers. The partners are I. M. Pei, Eason H. Leonard, and Henry N. Cabb. Work designed by ths firm includes Kips Bay Park Apartments, N. Y. C., Hyde Park Apartments, Chicago, and Place Ville Marie Development, Montreal.

PEREIRA & LUCKMAN, Los Angeles, Calif. William L. Pereira, FAIA, has been actively engaged in planning and architecture since 1931 when he first opened offices in Los Angeles and Chicago. Between 1931 and 1950 he became recognized as an authority on theater architecture and motion picture studio planning. In 1950 Pereira and Charles Luckman formed their planning-architectural-engineering firm. In 1958, this partnership was dissolved with each now operating his own offices.

PERKINS & WILL, Chicago, Ill. Founded in Chicago in 1935 by Lawrence B. Perkins, FAIA, and Philip Will, Jr., FAIA, this firm also has offices in White Plains, New York, and in Washington. In 1960, I.S.D., Inc., their interior space design division, was incorporated with offices in Chicago and New York City. In addition to a number of schools all over the country, the firm has designed office buildings and hospitals.

POHLMEYER & POHLMEYER, Fort Wayne, Ind. This firm is now known as Mox Pohlmeyer & Assoc. The principals are J. L. Sosenheimer, M. W. Pohlmeyer and C. J. Malott.

JAN HIRD POKORNY, New York, N. Y. Born in Czechoslovakia, Pokorny was educated in Prague and at Columbia University. He practiced in Czechoslovakia before opening his office in 1946 in New York, where his firm does industrial, residential, and college buildings. He is associate professor at Columbia School of Architecture and for three years was in charge of its Evening Division.

PRINZ & BROOKS, Dallas, Tex. Both Harold E. Prinz and LaVere Brooks are graduates of Texas A. and M. Prinz studied further at MIT and Brooks at the Art Institute of Chicago. Forming their firm in 1953, they have a record of such structures as the Earl Hayes residence, Parke-Davis Office and Warehouse in Dallas and the Boston Store, Bay Shore Center, Milwaukee.

RALPH RAPSON, Minneapolis, Minn. Rapson studied at the University of Michigan and Cranbrook Academy of Art. He was the head of the department of architecture of the Chicago Institute of Design (1942–46) and associate professor of architecture at MIT (1946-52), and is now head of the School of Architure, University of Minnesota. A winner of ten national competitions, his general architectural practice has included several embassies, churches, schools, and other building types.

ANTONIN RAYMOND & L. L. RADO, New York, N. Y., and Tokyo. This partnership was formed in 1944, and much of its work has been in Tokyo and the Far East. Raymond studied at the Polytechnic Institute, Prague; and Rado at the Technical University of Prague, and Harvard. Both are Fellows of the AIA.

JOHN LYON REID & PARTNERS, San Francisco, Calif. Reid, FAIA, received his education at the University of California. He formed the firm of John Lyon Reid & Partners in 1946, but is now a member of Reid, Rockwell, Banwell & Tarics.

ISIDOR RICHMOND AND CARNEY GOLDBERG, Boston, Mass. Richmond, FAIA, and Goldberg, FAIA, both studied at MIT and each had independent practices before entering this partnership following World War II. Buildings designed and executed by Richmond include housing developments, a chapel, schools, industrial structures, and a community center. Goldberg is well known for the many temples he has designed.

GEORGE T. ROCKRISE, San Francisco, Calif. Rockrise received his education at Syracuse and Columbia universities. Before starting his own practice in 1949, he worked for Edward Stone, the United Nations Headquarters Planning Commission, and for Thomas D. Church. In addition to a diversified practice, he has also lectured and taught at the University of California, the National University of Venezuela, Syracuse University, and Clemson College.

ROGERS, TALIAFERRO & LAMB, Baltimore, Md. Archibald C. Rogers and Francis T. Taliaferro formed original firm with Charles E. Lamb joining later as a partner. In addition to the Church of the Redeemer in Baltimore in which they collaborated with Pietro Belluschi, the firm has done such outstanding projects as: U. S. Embassy in Ciudad Trujillo, Downtown Plan for Hartford, Connecticut, and Harundale Mall Shopping Center south of Baltimore.

ISADORE ROSENFIELD, New York, N. Y. Rosenfield received his education at Harvard. After working with several prominent architectural firms, as well as the Department of Public Works in New York City, he became a partner in the firm of Isadore and Zachary Rosenfield, which collaborated with Kelly & Gruzen on design of the U. S. Veterans Administration Hospital, Wilkes-Barre. The firm has won recognition for its outstanding hospital work.

GEORGE VERNON RUSSELL, FAIA, Los Angeles, Calif. Russell was educated at California Institute of Technology and the University of Washington. He formed his present firm in 1950 and has received numerous national awards for his work. He is on the faculty of the University of Southern California and on the advisory committee of the College of Environmental Design, University of California.

MILTON A. RYAN, San Antonio, Tex. Ryan studied business administration at the state university, was later a bookkeeper for a lumber company, and finally became a registered architect in 1938, after extensive "on the job" experience. Predominantly, though not exclusively, he is a residential designer in San Antonio.

EERO SAARINEN & ASSOCIATES, Birmingham, Mich. Eero Saarinen, FAIA, principal partner of Eero Saarinen & Associates, was born in Finland and came to United States in 1923 with his father, the famous architect, Eliel Saarinen. He studied at Yale. Winner of numerous awards, Eero Saarinen is perhaps best known for such widely publicized work as his auditorium and chapel at MIT, the U. S. Embassy in London, the Trans World Airlines terminal at Idlewild, New York, the Dulles International Airport in Washington, and the Jefferson National Expansion memorial at St. Louis. He died in 1961.

MAX M. SANDFIELD, Dallas, Tex. Sanfield received his education at the University of Texas and MIT. His early practice was in New York and San Antonio, but in 1944 he moved to Dallas. He designed country clubs in Dallas and Washington, and many large homes in Texas and Arkansas.

SCHMIDT, GARDEN & ERIKSON, Chicago, Ill. This firm is prominently associated with the Chicago School, as the Bunte Candy Factory, Montgomery Ward & Company, the Chapin & Gore Building, etc. exemplify, and has in more recent years designed such outstanding buildings as the Veterans Research Hospital in Chicago, the American Hospital Association Building and others of equal distinction. Principals in the firm are Richard E. Schmidt, FAIA, Hugh M. G. Garden, FAIA, and Carl A. Erikson.

SHERLOCK, SMITH & ADAMS, Montgomery, Ala. This firm was organized in 1946 and incorporated in 1957. Moreland Griffith Smith, principal of the firm, is a fellow of the AIA. Mr. Richard Adams is deceased. Highlights of its activities include over eighty medical facilities; various Alabama banks and small office buildings; the Alabama Masonic Home Master Plan; college buildings; a courthouse; a library; and apartments.

SHERWOOD, MILLS AND SMITH, Stamford, Conn. The firm of Sherwood, Mills and Smith is directed by its seven partners: Thorne Sherwood, FAIA, Willis N. Mills, Lester W. Smith, Carrell S. McNulty, Thomas A. Norton, Gray Taylor, and Raymond Von Brock. The staff includes more than fifty architects, designers, and specialists. The firm's practice ranges from corporation offices, industrial plants, and college facilities, to hospitals, churches, and elementary and secondary schools.

SKIDMORE, OWINGS & MERRILL, New York, N. Y. The firm, founded in 1936, has sixteen general partners who direct the work in four principal offices – New York, Chicago, San Francisco, and Portland, Oregon. A staff of approximately 600 architects, engineers, and technicians provides complete domestic and international services in the fields of planning, design, engineering, and supervision of construction. Some of the firm's principal projects include the U. S. Air Force Academy, Lever House in New York, the Inland Steel Building in Chicago, the Crown Zellerbach Building in San Francisco and the master plan for Oak Ridge, Tennessee.

SMITH AND WILLIAMS, South Pasadena, Calif. Both Whitney R. Smith, FAIA, and Wayne R. Williams studied at the University of Southern California. Their partnership firm was formed in 1949 and has won numerous awards with a diversified practice including project housing, schools, military installations, recreational facilities, community buildings, union service centers, medical buildings, and commercial and industrial structures.

SMITH, HINCHMAN & GRYLLS, Detroit, Mich. This organization is a large architectural corporation with a long record of accomplishment. Its current officers are: Amedeo Leone, Robert F. Hastings, FAIA, L. J. Hosman, F. J. B. Sevald, and B. L. Miller. The firm is more than fifty years old and operates nationally and internationally. In addition to the home office in Detroit, it maintains a Canadian office.

RAPHAEL S. SORIANO, Tiburon, Calif. Soriano was born on Rhodes and became a United States citizen in 1930. His experience includes work with Richard Neutra and the Regional Planning Commission, County of Los Angeles. His private practice since 1934 has included such major projects as site planning, apartments, hospital, harbor facilities, research laboratories, office and medical buildings, and community centers. He is also currently doing research and development of industrialized package structures of aluminum, steel, paper, and plastics for international markets.

J. E. STANTON, Los Angeles, Calif. Stanton studied at Beaux-Arts and he collaborated with Pereira & Luckman on the design of the National Bureau of Standards Radio Laboratory, Boulder, Colorado. Since 1953 he has been in partnership with William F. Stockwell.

STEELE, SANDHAM & STEELE, Omaha, Neb. The firm has since 1956 practiced under the name of Steele, Sandham & Weinstein Co. Although Sandham retired in 1960, William L. Steele, Jr., and Alex Weinstein continue a general practice. As architects in association with two engineering firms, they recently designed and supervised construction of the new Federal Building and Post Office in Omaha.

STEVENS & WILKINSON, Atlanta, Ga. Preston S. Stevens, FAIA, was a principal in the firm of Burge & Stevens until 1946, and is now in partnership with James R. Wilkinson. Some of the major works of the firm are Georgia Baptist Hospital, Uncle Remus Library, Rich's Store for Men and the Wilby-Kensey Building.

EDWARD D. STONE, FAIA, New York, N. Y. Stone studied at the University of Arkansas, Harvard Architectural School, and MIT. He formed his firm in 1936. His practice is both national and international, covering such building types as hotels, universities, hospitals, and embassies; the best-known of his works are the U. S. Embassy in New Delhi and the U. S. Pavilion at the International Exposition in Brussels.

STONE AND MULLOY, MARRACCINI AND PATTERSON, San Francisco, Calif. Douglas D. Stone and Lou B. Mulloy together with Silvio P. Marraccini and Norman W. Patterson designed the Peninsula Memorial Blood Bank in San Mateo, California. The firm is now known as Stone, Marraccini & Patterson. Mulloy now has his office in Atherton, California.

STONE & PITTS, Beaumont, Tex. This firm was organized in 1934 as Stone & Pitts, reorganized in 1957 as Pitts, Mebane and Phelps. Principals of the firm are: Llewellyn William Pitts, FAIA, Mike Mebane, and Russell R. Phelps. Work includes projects for four major oil companies, a college, schools, a research center. It served as associated architects for the U. S. Embassy Building, Mexico City.

A. M. STRAUSS, Fort Wayne, Ind. He is principal of the firm A. M. Strauss, Inc., organized in 1949. He was associate architect on AIA award-winning U. S. Veterans Administration Hospital, Fort Wayne.

HUGH STUBBINS, JR., FAIA, Cambridge, Mass. Stubbins studied at the Georgia Institute of Technology and Harvard University. A member of the Department of Architecture at Harvard for 13 years, he served as its chairman in 1953. He has won numerous national and international honors. His practice is general, and includes such notable foreign work as the Congress Hall in West Berlin and the U. S. Consulate in Tangier.

PAUL THIRY, FAIA, Seattle, Wash. Thiry studied at École des Beaux-Arts, Fontainebleau, and the University of Washington. He organized his own firm in Seattle and has such buildings as the Church of Christ the King, Northeast Branch Public Library, Headquarters Building for Auburn General Depot to his credit.

THORSHOV & CERNY, Minneapolis and St. Paul, Minn. Robert G. Cerny and Roy N. Thorshov formed the firm of Thorshov & Cerny, which has now been dissolved. Cerny now has his own company of Cerny Associates, Inc., which carries on extensive work in architecture, engineering, and planning. Thorshov now has offices in Minneapolis.

TOOMBS, AMISANO & WELLS, Atlanta, Ga. Henry J. Toombs, FAIA, studied at University of Pennsylvania; Joseph Amisano was a Prix de Rome winner at Pratt Institute; and James Edwin Wells studied at Georgia Tech. Their partnership, organized in 1955, has engaged in a general practice. Their significant buildings include Georgia Warm Springs Foundation; Federal Reserve banks in Atlanta, Birmingham, Nashville, and Jacksonville; Oglethorpe University dormitories; and shopping centers in Cleveland, Tennessee, and Columbia, South Carolina.

TWITCHELL & RUDOLPH, Sarasota, Fla. Paul M. Rudolph, former member of the firm of Twitchell & Rudolph, received his education at Alabama Polytechnic Institute and Harvard. He has served as chairman of the department of architecture at Yale University since 1958. He organized his own firm in 1952 with offices in Sarasota, Cambridge, Massachusetts, and New Haven, Connecticut with principal works in residential, commercial, and institutional structures. Ralph S. Twitchell now has a private practice in Sarasota.

JOHN VAN DER MEULEN, Chicago, Ill. Van Der Meulen studied at the University of Michigan. He began his own architectural firm in 1946 after working several years in office of L. J. Sarvis. He has associated with Ralph Rapson on several projects such as the American Embassy in Stockholm and the U. S. Staff Apartment Buildings, Paris, for which AIA awards were given.

BRUCE M. WALKER, *see* KENNETH W. BROOKS

JASPER DUDLEY WARD, III, REGINALD CAYWOOD KNIGHT, New York, N. Y. Ward studied at MIT and gained design experience in the firm of Skidmore, Owings & Merrill. Knight studied at Syracuse, Columbia and Harvard universities. The partnership firm which they formed in 1949 was dissolved in 1951. Each has independent practice now—Ward in Louisville, Kentucky, and Knight in Sarasota, Florida.

JOHN CARL WARNECKE, San Francisco, Calif. The practice of John Carl Warnecke and Associates is the outgrowth of the independent practice Warnecke started in 1945 while employed as a designer in his father's office. The junior Warnecke founded his own firm in 1950 in San Francisco. The firm's work has received numerous awards and has been exhibited in museums of capital cities of Europe and Asia as well as in the United States.

WEED, JOHNSON ASSOCIATES, Miami, Fla. This firm, established by Robert Law Weed, FAIA, in 1922, was joined by Herbert H. Johnson in 1946. It has been responsible for a great variety of buildings, including, in the past few years, projects for the State Department, Allied Stores, Federated Stores, Sears, Roebuck and Co., International Minerals & Chemical Corp. and the First National Bank of Miami.

WEINBERG & TEARE, Cleveland, Ohio. Wallace G. Teare studied at Western Reserve University; Joseph L. Weinberg, FAIA, at Harvard. Their partnership firm was organized in 1950. They served as planning consultants to the Cleveland Rehabilitation Conservation Project, urban redevelopment pilot study, in 1945-46, and have executed such projects as PHA housing, shopping centers, and apartments.

JOHN P. WILTSHIRE AND J. HERSCHEL FISHER, Dallas, Tex. Wiltshire studied at the universities of Arkansas and Texas, and Fisher at the University of Texas and MIT. Their partnership was formed in 1946. Fisher has been, since 1955, partner in the architectural firm Fisher & Jarvis and Associates. Wiltshire now has his own firm.

WURSTER, BERNARDI AND EMMONS, San Francisco, Calif. Partners in the firm are William W. Wurster, FAIA, Theodore C. Bernardi and Donn Emmons. Wurster, the senior partner, studied at the University of California and, after several years of travel, opened his own office in 1926. Bernardi studied at the University of California also, while Emmons studied at Cornell and the University of Southern California. They became partners in the firm in 1944 and 1945 respectively. Although the early reputation of the group was won in the field of residential design, the practice has today become highly diversified.

L. MORGAN YOST, FAIA, Kenilworth, Ill. Yost was educated at Northwestern and Ohio State universities, and in 1949 was visiting professor of architecture at the University of Illinois. The work of his firm, in many different states, covers the design and construction of many individual homes as well as large-scale housing developments and factories, stores, and churches.

YOUNG, RICHARDSON, CARLETON & DETLIE, Seattle, Wash. The present firm of Young, Richardson & Carleton was founded in 1956, succeeding the partnership that dated from 1950. The firm has a general architectural and engineering practice, principally in the Seattle area, with collaborative partner participation.

INDEX

C

D

E

F

G

H

I

J

K

L

M

N

O

P

Q

R

S

T

U

V

W

X

Y

Z